MW00627875

The Good Steward Financial Empowerment Series

CPR FOR THE SOuL

Shawn D. Rochester, MBA

First Edition
ISBN 978-0-9990072-0-4

Written by Shawn D. Rochester, MBA

Produced and Published by Good Steward Publishing
Address P.O. Box 661, Southbury, CT 06488
Website www.goodstewardliving.com

DEDICATION

To my mother, Joyce, who sacrificed every
day to give my brother and me a better life,
in a land of opportunity.

To my aunt, Dorian, a brilliant, funny, selfless,
pioneering educator who transformed the lives
of thousands of students and mentored a
generation of educators.

To my aunt, Barbara, whose boundless love,
bright smile, hearty laugh, and generous
spirit helped to change my life.

To my wife, Delores, son Ethan, and daughter
Sarah, you are a gift from God and I love you
with all my heart.

CONTENTS

CHAPTER 4

Maximizing Your Household Cash Flow

CHAPTER 5

How to Allocate Cash Flow To Fund Ownership And Legacy

CHAPTER 6

Credit - The Good The Bad And The Ugly

CPR *for the* **SOuL**

INTRODUCTION

Would you like to increase your household cash flow by $200 to $1,500 per month, in a repeatable and sustainable fashion? How about adding $100,000 to over $1 million of income-generating assets to your retirement? What about being able to develop and execute a plan to eliminate *all of your household debt? This may not sound realistic but I assure you that it is achievable. I am a financial expert with decades of cash flow management and budgeting experience and my clients are living testimonies to the benefit of developing a mindset based on stewardship, ownership and legacy.*

I have spent years working with churches, community organizations, and businesses to develop The Good Steward Financial Empowerment Series in response to the resounding demand for financial knowledge and insight. This financial empowerment series is based on three powerful principles: stewardship, ownership, and legacy. *Stewardship is about helping our clients maximize their household cash flow by utilizing their resources to their highest and best use. Ownership is about finding the most effective ways to eliminate debt. Legacy is about helping our clients get on track to have enough resources to retire with security, be positioned to leave an inheritance, and have sufficient resources set aside so they can give generous-*

ly to those in need. I have helped countless families dramatically maximize their cash flow, eliminate their debt and leave a legacy not only for their children but also for their children's children.

My wife, Delores, and I founded Good Steward LLC (GSL), to provide financial education and advisory services based on these core principles and we have seen dramatic changes in our clients' lives. Since founding GSL, we've helped clients eliminate millions of dollars of debt and add tens of millions of assets to their retirement plans. Our workshop series teaches and employs our time-tested principles to help transform the lives of our students and clients and have a far-reaching, inter-generational impact.

We embarked on this journey several years ago when I attended a financial empowerment workshop sponsored by the men's ministry of a church. A lecturer was invited to do a financial presentation, and men from the church and throughout the community were invited to attend. Although the speaker was engaging and well-meaning, I thought the presentation lacked the necessary information to help the audience fully understand and address the many pressing financial issues that we so often face. Issues like how to increase household cash flow, eliminate debt, understand credit, develop a budget, and plan for one's future and future generations were not addressed. After the workshop, a few other attendees mentioned that they too would have liked more information on various aspects of personal financial management.

While the demand for financial wisdom was there, and the intention was clearly in the right place, it was sadly a missed opportunity. This workshop, and numerous others, exemplified one of the two concerns I have often had with much of the financial advice and education that is readily available to African-Americans. The financial advice and education either (1) doesn't address the fundamentals of wealth building, such as how to increase household cash flow, eliminate debt, understand credit, develop a budget, and plan for their future and their children's future or (2) it addresses problems that we don't have, e.g., how to allocate $1 million across various asset classes. Knowing how to allocate a million dollars would be a wonderful problem to have, but the vast majority of people aren't there yet, they're simply trying to figure out how to accumulate significant resources in the first place. This perpetual lack of financial wisdom, knowledge, and understanding is pervasive and many people are hungry for, and seeking, information and solutions to their monetary problems.

That's why I reached out to the ministry planning committee and offered to develop and deliver a transformative personal financial management workshop to their members. I was confident my decades of financial training could have a positive impact in our community. I had already helped business leaders of many Fortune 500 companies achieve their strategic and financial goals to develop and execute global strategies, invest billions in emerging businesses, and buy companies all over the world. This time, however, I wanted to help those who needed financial guidance and education the most. I have an intimate understanding of many of the challenges that people from meager beginnings face as they try to navigate their family through a myriad of financial obstacles. At that time, I'd already spent well over a decade developing a thorough financial management system for my family focused on stewardship, ownership, and legacy, which prioritized increasing cash flow and allocating it wisely, eliminating debt, funding retirement, and giving generously. The cumulative result of which enabled us to emerge from one of our worst economic downturns with more cash flow and greater wealth.

Finally, and most significant, I have always had a passion and conviction to share my knowledge with those who have the desire but lack the information to improve their financial situation. When my mother came to the United States from Barbados, she earned $150 a week working for wealthy families—cooking their meals and caring for their children. She would later go to school at night and receive a certificate in nutrition from Adelphi University while working as a food service supervisor at a major hospital in New York City. While she moved up the supervisory ranks and was an excellent saver, she didn't know anything about the power of 401k plans and the matching contributions that companies provided their employees or how much she was losing by using her checking and savings accounts for her long-term saving goals. Though she was motivated, she didn't know anyone who had already accumulated any real wealth and could coach her on how to maximize the little she had through investing, maximizing 401k plans, taking full advantage of tax benefits, and getting the most out of college savings plans. Unfortunately, the cost of not knowing and not getting sound financial advice translated into the loss of *hundreds of thousands of dollars in retirement assets and significantly limited her ability to provide the kind of inheritance she desperately wanted to leave to her children.*

I want to make sure that what happened to my mother doesn't happen to my family and to so many others. It can be intimidating to build a plan that puts your family on solid financial ground with limited financial knowledge and even less understanding of how wealth is accumulated and maximized. Often, the people who have financial understanding aren't connected to the people who most need it, and those who need it are forced to figure it out by themselves. It is a tough and lonely place to be, trying to figure it all out without a guide or mentor to help you navigate difficult financial decisions and provide a solid framework to help you accumulate resources. What do you do when there's nobody to help you fund college, help you get your first car, or help you put a down payment on a house? What do you do if you come from a family where, when somebody dies, you get a bill and not an inheritance? What do you do when you don't know anyone who has accumulated real wealth, you haven't been coached on what to do with the little you have now, and you're not sure how to get the most out of your circumstances when you do make more money? I know what it is like to graduate with student loan debt, to take on a mortgage, to make more money every year, yet feel like I had far less. I know what it's like to have a growing family, to do your best to help members of your extended family, and to forgo things that your friends and peers enjoy. And I also know what it's like to search through scripture long and hard for answers, for guidance, for perspective.

I created my financial empowerment workshop for people like my Mom. People who are self-motivated and predisposed to the concepts of stewardship, ownership, and legacy, and just need the knowledge and guidance to understand their finances and realize their economic goals. Personal financial management is not taught at school, or even at work. We usually learn how to handle money at home, either by watching our parents or actively learning by reading books or taking courses. The workshop was developed to address this gap in knowledge and understanding. It is based on the proven operating model and principles that I developed and refined over 20 years. Principles which help us to maximize the limited resources that we have, to maximize cash flow, to eliminate debt, and to set aside the necessary resources to give generously, and retire with dignity. These principles also empower us to be able to leave a substantial legacy for our children *and even their children. We designed the workshop with a scalable framework to help people dramatically improve their ability to manage, handle, and grow their limited resources.*

When I presented my first workshop at the men's ministry, I was blown away by how well it was received. At the end of the presentation I was overwhelmed with requests to offer it at other churches and organizations. Because of this need and positive outcome, I took the workshop on the road to a number of churches, retreats, and organizations and it evolved into a seminar, and eventually into an eight-hour financial education course called The Good Steward Financial Empowerment Series. The course arms participants with the wisdom, understanding, and knowledge necessary to dramatically improve their ability to become good stewards of their resources. It covers the principles of and frameworks for stewardship, ownership, and legacy. It is steeped in scripture, uniquely engaging, informative, and filled with practical actionable advice given in plain, but paradigm shifting language.

The response from the workshops were so overwhelming that many people sought me out to help them develop their own financial plans and to keep them accountable. Many institutions recognized its uniqueness and the significant need for this financial information and invited me to present it across the country. Because of this positive feedback, my wife and I decided to found a financial education and advisory company called Good Steward LLC. Like our Good Steward Empowerment Series, it focuses on stewardship, ownership, and legacy. As a reminder, stewardship is about helping our clients maximize their household cash flow by utilizing their resources to their highest and best use. Ownership is about finding the most effective ways to eliminate debt. Legacy is about helping our clients get on track to have enough resources to retire with security, be positioned to leave an inheritance for their children's children, and have sufficient resources set aside so they can give generously to those in need.

The results have been amazing, with our clients typically developing a plan to increase household cash flow by $200 to $1,500 per month, in a repeatable and sustainable fashion, and often adding $100,000 to $10,000,000 of income generating assets to their retirement. To reach a wider audience (and because of a lot of prompting from our clients and seminar attendees) we decided to publish a book based on our workshop series. That book is *CPR for the SOuL: How to Give Yourself a 20% Raise, Eliminate Your Debt, and Leave an Inheritance for Your Children's Children. In it are all the principles, frameworks, and tools to help you lay a foundation that will allow you to change the way you think about money, dramatically reduce your debt and increase your cash flow, better position yourself for retirement, and to leave a substantial legacy.*

CPR for the SOuL is a powerful financial empowerment tool. I hope you will immediately implement what you learn as you build or augment your financial empowerment plan.

CHAPTER 1

CPR FOR THE SOuL

There are forces at work that have sought to suffocate our entrepreneurial spirit, to snuff out our ability to develop healthy families, and to restrict our ability to develop communities that provide quality education, safe neighborhoods, and gainful employment. Worst of all, the combined effect of these forces has imbued us with a scarcity mentality and an environment that rewards us for putting our desire for short-term gratification, ahead of our need for long-term gain. These forces have had a corrosive effect on our SOuL, as individuals and as a community, and have made us a shadow of what we were meant to be. Take a look at these sobering statistics:

- Black Americans are 14% of the U.S. population but own 2%[i] of the total U.S. wealth

- Black families with college degrees have an average net worth that is the same as the average net worth of White families with less than a high school education

- 52% of Black borrowers in repayment on their student loans are either in default or serious delinquency[ii]

- The median net worth of White Americans in 2010 was 20 times the median net worth of Black Americans

- "… the average high-earning (top 25%) married Black household makes $83,741 a year, and has $91,782 in net wealth. The average low-earning (bottom 25%) married White household earns only $31,088 a year, and yet has $97,475 in assets—i.e., $5,6931 more[iii]"

- 35% of Black American households have a net worth of zero or less

- 37% of Black men ages 24 to 55 (prime working age) earn zero income

- Only 8% of Black American retirees are retired with financial security

- White Americans are five times more likely to get an inheritance than African-Americans

- White Americans' inheritance is 10 times larger than the average African-American inheritance

- 91% of White Americans' inheritance goes to increase wealth vs. just 20% for African-Americans

If you are shocked by these statistics, that's understandable, because they are shocking and often not discussed. If you believe that it puts Black Americans at a severe disadvantage, you're right. However, regardless of the little that we currently have, or the cause of our situation, we should focus on using our limited resources to their highest and best use and be willing to sacrifice short-term gratification for long-term transformation. To do that, we're going to have to resuscitate one of the most important aspects of our economic well-being—we're going to need to apply CPR to our SOuL. What is CPR for the SOuL? Let's start with what CPR is and then we'll talk about what we mean by SOuL.

WHAT IS CPR?

The "C" in CPR stands for "Our Charge" which means to seek and apply wisdom, knowledge, and understanding in order to maximize our resources and leave an inheritance for our children's children[iv]. This Charge is derived from Proverbs in the Old Testament and is quite profound. I remember when I first read about leaving an inheritance for my children's children and how daunting it seemed. It was sobering to realize that all the effort I was exerting to put myself and my family in a good financial position, though necessary, was not sufficient. That as a "good" man, I am supposed to leave an inheritance for my children's children. The enormity of that hit me like a ton of bricks and made me think deeply about what was meant by inheritance. Over time it became clear that they were really talking about two things. The first is a good name. In our communities, we understand this instinctively. Oh, you're such and such's boy, or such and such's girl. People say that because where you come from matters and "who" you come from matters. It means that you come from a family that's had an impact in your community and there is strong expectation that you are going to live up to that impact. That's the first kind of inheritance, a good name for your children to live up to. The second kind is about resources— about leaving assets for future generations to build on. That's one of the things that separates us from our counterparts, the enormous head start that other communities have in terms of resources that were put in place by past generations to help this current generation get a head start in life.

Since our Charge requires us to use wisdom, knowledge, and understanding to manage our current resources and put ourselves in a position to leave an inheritance, a natural question is what do you mean by wisdom, knowledge, and understanding? Let's start with wisdom, which is really quite simple. Wisdom is the accumulation of understanding over time.

There is an African proverb that says when an old man or old woman dies, a library burns to the ground. This powerful proverb describes the incredible amount of information and experience that is lost when an elder passes away. In the days of old, wisdom was said to be more valuable than gold[v] and people were counseled to spare no expense in acquiring it. If that sounds strange, think of it this way: if you are unwise (i.e. a fool), it does not matter how much money you have now, because you won't have it for long. Why? Because your lack of understanding will ultimately cause you to lose what you have. Hence, the saying, "a fool and his money will always part." While that saying is true, experience has taught me that a fool and his money were very fortunate to have known each other in the first place.

If wisdom is the accumulation of understanding over time, then what is understanding? Understanding is the application of knowledge (the facts, information, and skills that you acquire through experience or education) to help you live a "good" and "just" life. "Good" is in relationship to God. "Just" refers to your relationship with your fellow man (your brothers and sisters on earth). Therefore, the extent to which we act in ways that demonstrate that we (1) love our neighbors as we love ourselves or (2) treat others the way we want to be treated, shows our understanding.

Understanding is so important that scripture says, "with all thy getting, get understanding[vi]" and that a home, which is the primary building block of a community, is established through understanding[vii].

To seek and apply wisdom, knowledge, and understanding in order to maximize our limited resources and leave an inheritance for our children's children, may seem quite daunting or downright scary, which is why we supplement our efforts with Prayer, which is the "P" in CPR. It's a Prayer of Empowerment that you recite before, during, and after your most challenging times on this journey. When you have done all that you can, and when you have gotten to the end of yourself, it's important to remember that it's at that point when God's work is completely and unmistakably clear. The Prayer of Empowerment is as follows:

> *Lord strengthen us for we are weary*
> *and increase our power for we are weak.*
> *Allow us to put this knowledge into practice*
> *and rise like the Phoenix from our current*
> *situation, to transform our lives and the lives*
> *of our families and to be a blessing to those*
> *who are the least, last and left out. Amen*

Last, but certainly not least, the "R" in CPR stands for Responsibility. While we are in the undesirable position of having very limited resources, scripture says that if you can be trusted with little, you can also be trusted with much. Therefore, our responsibility is to demonstrate that we can be trusted with the little that we have, so that we will be prepared for the overflow that is coming. The word "responsibility," while used frequently, is often misunderstood. At the end of the day, taking responsibility is about accepting that what is required of you is more important than what is desired by you. When we talk about applying CPR, we are talking about applying our Charge, our Prayer of Empowerment, and taking Responsibility.

WHAT IS SOuL?

The next step is to understand what we mean by SOuL. SOuL is an acronym for Stewardship, Ownership, and Legacy. The central idea is that stewardship leads to ownership and ownership ultimately leads to legacy.

So, what is Stewardship? Stewardship is about getting the highest and best use out of your limited resources. It is about maximizing your household cash flow because, without cash flow, there's no savings, no assets, no investments, and no wealth to pass on. It's also about using your gifts and abilities to generate a significant return on your limited resources.

Whoever can be trusted with little can also be

trusted with much, and whoever is dishonest with little will be dishonest with much. So, if you have not been trustworthy in handling worldly wealth, who will trust you with true riches? And if you have not been trustworthy with someone else's property who will give you property of your own[viii]?

The scripture above, from Luke 16:10-12 NIV, is worth reflecting on because we can easily become so focused on storing up treasures in heaven that we lose sight of managing the treasures we have in this life. It's easy to forget that (1) what we do with what we have today, affects the treasures we're going to have in the hereafter, (2) how we manage other people's property today will ultimately determine how much property we get of our own, and (3) how we manage our own property will determine if we get to keep it. This is what we mean when we say stewardship leads to ownership.

Now, while we often instinctively understand the idea of Ownership, what I'm talking about is outright ownership, or full ownership. This means you are the only person who has a claim on your assets. That's what people mean when they say they own something "free and clear." It means "free and clear" of any outside claims. So, full ownership requires the elimination of all claims to your assets, which in turn maximizes the amount of cash flow available to you. Where do these outside claims come from? They often arise as a result of having debt.

When you borrow money, the lender will usually establish a claim on your assets equal to the amount you owe them. Considering that 23% of the average African-American income is spent servicing debt (i.e., making principal and interest payments), we need to develop realistic and actionable plans to eliminate every dollar of debt that we have in the shortest possible time. This is important because we cannot leave the kind of legacy that we are required to if almost a quarter of our income is consumed by debt. For ownership to ultimately lead to legacy, we must eliminate our debt to maximize our cash flow.

Legacy, on the other hand, is about (1) positioning yourself to leave an inheritance for your children's children, (2) having enough resources to retire with dignity and (3) proactively setting aside money so you can help people who are in need.

If you want to maximize your ability to help those in need, you're going to have to proactively and intentionally set aside resources so you can act on that need when you see it. This allows you to be able to do more than just pray for a person in need or only offer them kind words. It's about being able to sow directly into that need when you see it and to do so in a selfless way. Setting aside resources in advance allows you to align your desire to do good with your ability to do so.

When we talk about applying CPR to our SOuL, we are talking about applying our charge, our Prayer of Empowerment, and taking responsibility to resuscitate our commitment to stewardship, ownership, and, ultimately, legacy. It's about rejecting anything that inhibits our ability to leave a legacy, like accumulating too much debt and unnecessary consumption, and continually doing more of the things that allow us to leave a legacy, like spending our resources wisely, quickly paying off debt, and taking advantage of tax deferred retirement plans. This takes discipline and focus and a new way of thinking. It requires a new mindset, one that is focused on stewardship, ownership, and legacy.

CHAPTER 2

The Six Principles For
Financial Success

ny successful endeavor in life requires that
we follow certain principles. These principles help to keep us focused and on track
regardless of the obstacles we encounter
or the terrain that we traverse. As you embark on this
journey to financial empowerment, it is important that
your actions be grounded in certain principles that
will help you achieve your goals and avoid common
pitfalls. In this chapter, we explore six key principles
for financial success: The Matthew Principle, The Airline Safety Principle, Think Differently, Work and Persistence, Be a Blessing, and Context and Environment
Matter. These principles will help to lay an important
foundation that you will build on throughout the book.

1 | THE MATTHEW PRINCIPLE

Matthew Principle means that (all other things being equal) you are given resources according to your financial ability (not your righteousness) and that you are expected to deliver a significant return on the limited resources that you possess. The Matthew Principle comes from the Parable of the Talents[ix], which is one of my favorite parables. The Parable of the Talents is about a master who is about to go on a long journey and gives three of his servants resources—according to their several abilities to manage—while he is away. He gives the first servant five talents, the second two talents and the third one talent, then he sets out on a long journey.

While the master is away, the first servant takes the five talents he was given, goes and trades them, and doubles his talents. The second servant goes out and also doubles his talents. The third servant takes his talent and buries it in the ground for safe keeping. After a long time, the master returns and summons each servant to give an account of the talents that he was given.

The first servant arrives and says, "Master you gave me five talents and I have produced five more." The master says, "Well done, good and faithful servant, you have been faithful with a few things and I will put you in charge of much more, come and enjoy what your master has to offer." The second servant arrives and says, "Master you gave me two talents and I have pro-

CPR FOR THE SOuL

duced two more." The master says, "Well done, good and faithful servant, you have been faithful with a few things and I will put you in charge of much more, come and enjoy what your master has to offer."

The third servant arrives and says, "Master you gave me one talent and I buried it in the ground to keep it safe. I did this because I know that you are a harsh man, reaping where you have not sown and gathering where you have not thrown straw. Here is the talent that you gave me." The master looks at him and says, "You are a wicked and slothful servant. If you knew that I am a harsh man, that I reap where I have not sown and gather where I have not thrown straw, then why didn't you at least give the talent to the money changers so you could get interest?" Then the master says, "Take the talent from this servant and give it to the servant who has 10 talents. For whoever has, will be given more and they will have abundance and whoever does not have, even what they have will be taken away. Now take that wicked servant, and throw him into the darkness, where there will be weeping and gnashing of teeth."

That is a deep scripture that gives you a lot to think about. I had to meditate on it many times because I thought the punishment was too harsh. The third servant was just trying to keep the money safe until the master's return, but he received a swift and severe punishment for his actions. The master did not even take a couple of days to think about it, his judgment was immediate and final. But why was the punishment so severe? It was just one talent. I mean, what's the big deal? As I reflected on it and did some research, I started to truly understand the lesson. I realized that the master called his servants according to their several abilities. Several is just a fancy word for individual. Each servant was given resources according what he could handle, manage, and grow.

This is where we tend to get confused, because we usually think of people being called according to their righteousness, but these servants were called according to their ability. Being righteous is important but that doesn't mean that you have the ability to manage resources. The first servant was chosen because he had the ability to handle, manage, and grow the five talents he was given. The second and third servants were also chosen because they had the ability to handle, manage, and grow the talents they received. The second servant took his two talents and used his ability to double his master's money. The problem with the third servant is that while he had the ability to handle, manage, and grow the one talent that he was given, he chose not to. This is why the master called him both wicked and slothful. Think about it. He didn't even do the bare minimum, which was to give it to the money changers who would have paid him interest to use the talent. Notice that the first and second servant received the same reward and it was far larger than the few talents they were initially given.

While those points are somewhat illuminating, I still struggled with the severity of the punishment because, whether it was five talents, two talents, or one talent, it just didn't seem like it was that big of a deal. How much was a talent anyway? It sounds like it's just a couple of bucks or a few gold coins. When I researched how much a talent was I got quite a surprise. A talent is not just a couple of bucks or a few gold coins, a talent is equivalent to what you would pay someone for 20 years[x] of labor. Think about it this way: the average American household income in 2015 was $55,775[xi] per year. For the average American household, the equivalent of one talent would be $1,116,000. That is a large sum of money. It's as if the first, second, and third servants were given a total of $8,924,000; $5,578,000, $2,231,000, and $1,116,000, respectively. Can you imagine being given that kind of money and having the ability to double it and then not doing so? Can you imagine burying it in the ground and not putting the money to work to generate interest? That's crazy.

Now you can see why that did not go over well with the master and why the punishment was so swift and severe. The best that you can say about the third servant is that his desire was to keep the talent safe, because the master was a harsh man. But what was required of him, was to use his ability to handle, manage, and grow it and he didn't.

The Matthew Principle tells us that (all things being equal) when it comes to resources, it's about ability, not righteousness. Therefore, regardless of your desire, you have a responsibility to deliver a significant return on what you have. If not, at the end of the day it will be taken away from you and shifted to those with more ability. The key here is ability and responsibility. Many people ask for more resources but are not prepared to handle, manage, and grow them. If you want more resources, you must first increase your ability to handle more resources and understand that, when you get those resources, you are required to use your abilities to deliver a significant return on them.

You must also remember that, all things being equal, resources always flow from those with low ability to those with high ability. Let's look at a couple of examples. If I were to ask you to think of people who have low financial ability and lots of resources, I bet you would probably think about lottery winners. We've all heard about how the vast majority of them end up broke within a few years of coming into a massive amount of money. You might also think of professional athletes because we've also heard stories about NFL and NBA players winding up broke or in financial distress within a few years of retiring. Consider the 2016/2017 NBA season, for example.

During that season, the NBA was contractually required to distribute $3 billion[xii] to 450 players, 60%[xiii] of whom will likely be broke or in financial distress a few years after they retire. This is very sad because it means they are effectively just "pass through" entities. The money flows into and out of their hands, with no lasting impact, no transformation, and no legacy. I'm sure you can think of many entertainers who've also made and lost massive fortunes and are now broke and struggling.

The problem, however, is not only with lottery winners, professional athletes, and entertainers. It happens with ordinary folks as well. Let's look at a 30-year period between 1980 to 2010, to see what happened to high net worth Americans (i.e., the top 20%), the medium net worth Americans (i.e., the middle 80%) and the low net worth Americans (i.e., the bottom 20%). It turns out that the wealth of the high net worth folks went up by 120% during that period. That's like doubling your net worth and then adding another 20% on top of it. What about the folks in the middle range, what happened to them? Their wealth went up by about 13%. Now, you might be tempted to say, that's not bad but we're talking about 13% over a 30-year period[xiv]. Thirty-plus years ago, you could go to the movies with $5, catch a matinee and get a lunch special at a fast-food restaurant. You can't do that now because the price of everything has gone up – this is what we call inflation.

Taking inflation into account, the wealth of the folks in the middle range is actually worth less than it was at the beginning of the 30-year period. What about the folks in the bottom range of 20%? Unfortunately, their average wealth fell below zero during that period. That's a massive shift in resources over time. Is it that these folks are not good people? Is it that they are not hardworking or righteous? No. Not at all. What's the difference? It's partly because financial ability is tilted toward the higher net worth folks who have the resources to hire advisors to give them insights on how to best manage and grow their resources. It is also because the economic landscape heavily favors the wealthy. Just as important, it is because you can receive 12 to 20 years of education and never formally learn the skills that are necessary to effectively manage your limited resources. One way or another, we should all learn about money management and wealth building and actively develop those skills because, as we've seen with lottery winners, professional athletes, and entertainers, we live in a society that punishes people when their resources increase faster than their ability to manage them.

2 | THE AIRLINE SAFETY PRINCIPLE

The second principle is the Airline Safety Principle. It means that you cannot be an effective help to others if you do not have a strong financial core. On an airplane, right before takeoff, the flight attendant tells you where the exits are and how to get out of the plane if there's a crash landing. He also tells you that if there is a loss of cabin pressure, a mask will drop down in front of you to provide you with oxygen. What he tells you to do next with the mask is of the utmost impor-

"Before you can be an effective help to others, you've got to ensure that you are in a strong position yourself. Otherwise, not only will you not be of use, but you may also find yourself in the same position as those you are trying to save."

tance. He tells you to put the mask on first. He does not say to put it on your husband, your wife, your mom or dad, or even your children first. Why? Because you're of no use to anyone if you're without oxygen. The Airline Safety Principle means that, before you can be an effective help to others, you've got to ensure that you are in a strong position yourself. Otherwise, not only will you not be of use, but you may also find yourself in the same position as those you are trying to save.

Have you ever heard of a keystone? It's the center stone in an arch bridge. These types of bridges have been in use for thousands of years and are one of the greatest innovations of the ancient world. An arch bridge has a large stone in the center. That stone is the keystone because it locks and holds all the other stones in place. The design is so strong that in ancient times they didn't even need mortar or concrete to construct it. You could build a stone bridge like that today and drop a bus on it, and it's going to be fine. The piece that holds it together is the keystone.

Ever heard of a cornerstone? A cornerstone concept is derived from the first stone set in the construction of a foundation that all other stones are set in relation to. It's vitally important because, if the cornerstone is not properly set, the entire structure will be out of alignment.

I've never built a house but I've paid for a house to be built. I know that if you don't get the foundation right, every angle in the house will be off. It's going to be a real disaster because your roof won't fit right and, no matter how beautiful you try to make the rooms, the framework will be out of alignment. Keystones and cornerstones are vitally important to creating a strong and securely aligned foundation. What I want you to know is that in your family, you're the keystone and the cornerstone. If you're not in a strong and secure financial position, everything else will be insecure and out of alignment. This is why it is imperative that you are in a strong financial position first, so you can be an effective help to others.

Consider this: if you want to knock a building down, what do you do? Do you randomly throw things at it? No, you could do that, and make a lot of noise, but the building is still going to be standing. If you want to bring a building down quickly and efficiently, focus on its crucial load-bearing structures, because those structures carry the weight of the entire building. Once you remove them, the whole building comes tumbling down. Those structures are like the keystone and the cornerstone, like you and me. That's the principle.

> *I must study politics and war that my sons may have liberty to study mathematics and philosophy. My sons ought to study mathematics and philosophy, geography, natural history, naval architecture, navigation, commerce, and agriculture, in order to give their children a right to study painting, poetry, music, architecture, statuary, tapestry, and porcelain.*
> — *John Adams*

The above quote is truly profound. John Adams is talking about laying a solid foundation so that his children will be in a position to build the next level of the house. Then their children will be able to build on top of that firm ground. If we want our children to prosper and be in a position to help others, we've got to lay a solid economic foundation for them to build on so they can become a more effective help to others and their children can build on it.

3 | THINK DIFFERENTLY

The third principle is to think differently because you cannot solve today's challenges with yesterday's thinking. Scripture says we should be transformed by the renewing of our minds. This means that we must strive to think differently. This journey requires that we develop new habits and routines and a mindset that is consistently based on stewardship, ownership and legacy. In the US and around the world, companies spend billions of dollars on advertising to influence us to consume an ever-increasing amount of their products. The money spent on advertising in the US is $190 billion and around the world the number is closer to $600 billion annually. Companies spend this money because they know that we are predictable, impulsive, and unaware of the subconscious cues that help trigger a desire for certain products or services. These companies have spent billions on research and are very aware of what is attractive to us. Think about it. Would you spend almost $200 billion on something you didn't think was going to work? Would you spend it year after year if you didn't know it was already working? Of course, not. This is why so many people fail when it comes to stewardship—they simply don't realize that there's a massive system working against them and they don't have a system that's working for them.

Unfortunately, consumer education is not a priority for most companies because it's not in their best interest to empower you to consume less. Let's take the financial services industry for example, while they spend $17 billion annually to sell various services, they only spend about $30 million a year on the direct provision of financial education. Yes, you read that correctly, they spend $17 billion to get you to buy stuff and $30 million so you can understand what you're doing. So, for every $570 they spend to get you to buy something, they're spending $1 so you will be well informed when making those buying decisions.

Consider the automotive industry. Ford, Chrysler, General Motors, and the other car makers spend a lot of money to get customers to buy their cars, but do not spend much money on consumer education. However, the state you live in has an interest in you being able to properly use your vehicle. If you want to be able to drive your car, you're going to have to demonstrate that you understand the rules of the road and that you drive in a safe and effective manner. Otherwise, you're not going to be allowed to drive in those states. This is one of the reasons why the auto industry spends money on consumer information; to make certain that you can drive the car they want to sell you. That creates somewhat of a balance in that industry, but there isn't much of a balance in many other industries.

While you can certainly understand why companies

are not very motivated to educate us to become better consumers, the real question is, are we doing enough to educate ourselves to be able to make the best buying decisions? The answer is no, because African-American households spend less than 2% of their income on education in general and far less on consumer education in particular. This is detrimental because when you are trying to chart a new financial course and develop a new way of thinking, a lack of information and education makes it difficult to gain ground against the powerful headwinds that try to push you back to old ways of thinking.

> *Your beliefs become your thoughts.*
> *And your thoughts become your words.*
> *And your words become your actions.*
> *And your actions become your habits.*
> *And your habits become your values.*
> *And your values become your destiny.*
> — *Mahatma Gandhi*

This powerful quote from Mahatma Gandhi means that if you want to change someone's destiny, you can do it by changing their belief system. This changes their thoughts, their actions, their habits, and their values. It is a tool that can be used to influence us positively or negatively. This brings me back to the $190 billion being spent annually on advertising. That money is being spent to influence your belief system about consumption (i.e., stewardship—buying things we don't need, with money we don't have) which subsequently affects our destiny (i.e., ownership and legacy).

This is where the principle of Think Differently comes into play. We cannot act differently, until we think differently and we are not going to think differently until we have a new belief system or mindset, one that is focused on stewardship, ownership, and legacy and represents something greater than ourselves and consumerism. This is why the idea of focusing on your SOuL is so important.

4 | WORK AND PERSISTENCE

The fourth principle is related to work and persistence because there is no shortcut to success; hard work and persistence are key. The minute someone tells you about a quick fix when it comes to financial management, you should discount what they are saying and move on. There's no such thing as a quick financial fix. It's like when we think someone is an overnight success. It might seem that way but being successful, in any field, often means spending thousands of hours honing a craft. The amount of work that we see someone doing is always just a tiny fraction of the work that has already been done. Success requires effort because a significant amount of work goes into building something great.

People often throw around the word "work" without truly understanding how profound and important it is. Think about it this way: work existed before faith, before sin, and before life. That sounds deep, right? And you might think, "hang on a minute, I don't remember reading that in scripture," but if you go back to Genesis, the first words are "In the beginning," and then it describes what God was doing over the course of seven days. God created and spoke things into existence over the course of the first six days and on the seventh day, He rested from his work. When He was working on the first and second days, there was no life, because life did not start until the third day. So, work existed before life. But what about faith?

When Adam was in Eden, he saw God face to face. You and I don't see God face to face. That's why we need to have faith in God. We must have faith that He is there and that He has our back in all our situations. Adam didn't have to do that. Adam saw God face to face. He did not need to have faith. So, work existed before faith. What about before sin? Scripture says, "The Lord took the man and put him in the garden to work it and take care of it." So, well before Adam and Eve ignored the explicit instructions that led to their fall, there was work—and after their fall, the work became more intense and difficult. So, work existed before sin.

Sometimes, we like to substitute prayer and faith

for the work that must be done. Prayer is done before, during, and after any task or endeavor. Faith is what you have when you've been assured of victory, even if it seems like you won't get it, you push forward anyway, based on faith. It is important to remember that faith is not action, it's what accompanies inspired action.

What good is it, my brothers and sisters, if someone claims to have faith, but no deeds? Can faith save them?

".....so many people fail when it comes to stewardship—they simply don't realize that there's a massive system working against them and they don't have a system that's working for them."

… Suppose a sister or brother is without clothes and daily food. If one of you says to them, Go in peace, keep warm, and be well-fed. But does nothing about their physical needs, what good is it? … Faith without works is like a body without a spirit. – James 2:14 -16 & 26 NIV

Like a body without a spirit, that's profound and very clear. Work and actions are the manifestation of your faith. Work is also front-end loaded. That means you've got to put in a ton of it before you see the fruits of your labor. If you've ever worked on a farm, you know how much work has to be done long before you get a harvest. It's an incredible amount of backbreaking effort. If you operate based only on what you see, you'd abandon your crops long before you would reap a bountiful harvest.

That's where persistence comes in. Persistence is the ability to keep pushing, fighting and working long before you see the rewards. This quote from Calvin Coolidge illustrates the importance of persistence:

> *Nothing in this world can take*
> *the place of persistence.*
> *Talent will not: nothing is more common*
> *than unsuccessful men with talent.*
> *Genius will not; unrewarded genius is*
> *almost a proverb. Education will not: the*
> *world is full of educated derelicts. Persistence*
> *and determination alone are omnipotent.*

All things being equal, the person who decides to do something and sticks to it, is the person who wins. That's what I tell my children, every single day. My children are runners who love to compete in track and field races. My daughter has two Nutmeg state records in her age group. She is doing well and decided she could rest on her laurels.

" I asked her, "Do you remember last year when we were watching another little girl who was beating everyone?"

She said, "Yes, Daddy."

"And what did you say?" I asked her.

"I said I wanna be like her."

"So, we practiced and worked hard so you could be like her right?"

"Yes, Daddy," she answered.

"Well, I'm telling you that somebody saw you winning all of those races and they said, 'I wanna be like her.' And they're practicing right now to beat you."

She looked me in the eye and said, "They ain't going to beat me."

I replied, "If you're resting on your laurels, not working and not practicing, and not persisting, then they will surely beat you."

She got the message and kept putting in the work."

5 | BE A BLESSING

The fifth principle is to be a blessing to those in need. This principle is simple: when God blesses you with resources and you in turn decide to be a blessing to someone else, He will honor you. "A generous man will himself be blessed, for he shares his food with the poor." – Proverbs 22:9. This is a powerful act because he does not have to be generous, but he does so anyway.

To be able to give generously to the poor, to be a blessing to those in need, you must have an abundance of resources. When Jesus sent his disciples out, he told them to, "take nothing for the journey"—no staff, no bag, no bread, no money, no extra shirt — "whatever house you enter, stay there until you leave that town." The people who received them provided for them while they were in town. When the disciples were hungry, their hosts did not say, "Be ye fed." They provided for their hunger. If the disciples needed clothes, their hosts did not say, "be ye clothed." They provided them with clothing, gave them room and board, and took care of them.

Have you ever wondered how a few of Jesus's followers, or Galileans, or followers of the Way, survived the early years of persecution and grew, over time, into more than 2 billion people today? How did that happen? While we know that in later periods, military conquests, colonialism, high birth rates and other factors clearly played a significant role, we know very little about what happened in the early years when they appeared to be just another "strange" group of believers. What was it about these people, these strange Galileans? Well, one of the peculiar things about them was that they were exceedingly generous and selfless, which was quite unusual 2,000 years ago in the Roman Empire.

Their generosity was so impactful that the Roman Emperor, Julian, had to send a letter to the high priest of Galatia urging the distribution of grain and wine to the poor, noting that "the impious Galileans [Christians], in addition to their own, support ours [and] it is shameful that our poor should be wanting our aid." He was basically saying, "Yo, what's going on here? These Galileans, are being more generous to our poor than we are." And he told the high priest to do something about it. Why? Because when you are a blessing to those in need and they don't expect it, it causes them to see things differently. And if you're an emperor of a vast land, which is held by force, you don't want large numbers of people "thinking differently."

Thinking differently makes a difference. It causes cognitive dissonance. Cognitive refers to how you think. Dissonance means there's a problem with the thinking. It happens when, you have an expectation about the world and then you see something and it does not meet that expectation. Afterward, you cannot function until you get rid of that dissonance. That is what happens when someone is generous to people who don't expect it and also don't ask for anything in return. It makes people wonder, "why would you do that? I don't even like you. As far as I knew you didn't even like me." And it can lead to a powerful conversation about why you would do such a thing. Even if it doesn't, the fact of the matter is, people feel more like being a blessing to others when something unexpected and positive happens to them. When we bless others, we create a chain of events that can lead to those people blessing others. Sadly, we are all used to disappointment and we protect ourselves by being ready for it, but we are rarely ever ready for selfless generosity.

At the end of the day, being a blessing to others is a manifestation of your faith. Your children see it and they emulate it. God sees it and He rewards you for it. There's a South African proverb that says, "Abundance does not spread. Poverty does." As you gain abundance do your best to help spread it.

6 | CONTEXT AND ENVIRONMENT MATTER

The sixth principle is an important one that shows how context and environment matter, because they either multiply or reduce the efforts of your hard work. Consider the parable below:

A farmer went out to plant some seeds. As he scattered them across his field, some fell in a foot path, and the birds came and ate them. Others fell on shallow soil with underlying rock. Seeds sprouted quickly, because the soil was shallow. But the plants soon wilted under the hot sun. And since they didn't have deep roots, they died. Other seeds fell amongst the thorns, and grew up and choked. Still others fell on fertile soil, and they produced a crop that was 30, 60, even 100 times as much as had been planted. – Matthew 13:3-8 NIV

What a powerful and profound parable. What resonates with me is that the same seed fell on four different environments. It was the same seed, the same Word, the same work, the same wisdom, the same effort, but the difference was the environment on which it fell. Environment matters because it can have a multiplier effect on the work and effort that happens within it. It can either dramatically increase or decrease the yield that your efforts produce. In Outliers: The Story of Success, Malcolm Gladwell writes that the three most important factors to someone's ultimate success are (1) where you are born (2) when you are born (3) who you know. Each of those factors represents an important aspect of your environment. According to Gladwell:

> *People don't rise from nothing... they are invariably the beneficiaries of hidden advantages and extraordinary opportunities and cultural legacies that allow them to learn and work hard and make sense of their world in ways others cannot... it's not enough to ask what successful people are like... it is only by asking where they are from that we can unravel the logic behind who succeeds and who doesn't.*

People rarely overcome their environments, they are instead products of those environments. You don't send your child to Harvard to overcome the environment at Harvard, you send them there, because of what that environment produces. You want them to be a product of it, to be nourished by it and to thrive in it. Therefore, when someone tells you about how hard they worked, you should consider the environment in which that work was done.

Think about it this way. It's like being tasked to grow corn in an arid environment. While you may have the best seeds from the most productive crops, are you really going to get a bountiful yield? The answer is no. Why? Because arid environments lack the moisture

///

We must create an environment where the outcomes we want for ourselves and our children can be manifested.

///

and mineral content necessary to provide a bountiful yield. You can work incredibly hard in that environment and get more than what others might have gotten, but you will never be able to produce as much as you could have if your environment was more fertile. How about if you were tasked with growing corn in the deep, rich, soil of the US Great Plains, are you going to get a bountiful yield? Absolutely. If you apply the same work and effort in that environment, you will get completely different results.

If we're not careful and cognizant of the role that

environment plays, we might end up blaming the seeds or the farmer for the meager outcome. Criticizing the farmer in the arid environment and praising the farmer in the fertile environment is what happens when we compare outcomes without considering the environment.

So yes, work is indeed critical and it must be done and we must persist in it, but we must be conscious of the environment in which it is done. We must be cognizant of the environment in which our children are working. Are they going to receive a bountiful yield when they put in the work? Are they going to receive the same reward when they put in the same amount of work as others? We must create an environment where the outcomes we want for ourselves and our children can be manifested. That process is called terraforming, which is altering an environment so it's more conducive to your success.

Picture two environments. One is verdant with rolling hills and valleys. It is full of resources and opportunities. The other is an arid desert of harsh terrain with little water or resources to sustain greenery, or fruit-bearing trees. Which environment do you think is going to have a positive multiplier effect on our actions? Which environment is our children living in? Which environment represents the state of our communities? I think you know the answer. Unfortunately, our yield is often measured without taking our environment into consideration.

What's wrong with you? You've only produced three bushels. You need to deliver 10 bushels. Get to 10 bushels and we can talk. Go back and work harder." You work hard, and produce five bushels, an almost 70% increase over your initial efforts. "Five bushels! Didn't I tell you I need 10? Don't you understand? Am I not being clear? I'm consistently getting 10 bushels from others. What's wrong with you? Why don't you work harder?" Hard work is not the problem. *There is no shortage of hardworking people in this world, the problem is that there is a shortage of productive environments that have a positive multiplier effect on their work.*

❝ When I was younger, I heard a joke about a scientist experimenting on a frog. In the experiment, the scientist would scream *"jump"* at the frog, measure how high the frog jumped, and then amputate one of the frog's legs. After each leg was amputated, he noticed that the frog did not *jump* as high as it had before the amputation. Finally, after all of the frog's legs had been removed, the scientist yelled *"jump,"* but the frog did not jump. The scientist yelled "jump" again and again but the frog still did not jump. Finally, the scientist concluded that after all the frog's legs were removed the frog became deaf. The lesson here is that if you're focused on outcomes and not context, you're always going to come to the wrong conclusion."

CHAPTER 3

Goal-Setting And Understanding Your Cash Flow

An average person with average talents and ambition, and average education, can outstrip the most brilliant genius in our society, if that person has clear, focused goals.
— *Mark Kay Ash*

LET'S TALK ABOUT GOALS

What are goals anyway? Goals are objectives you would like to achieve within a certain amount of time. The key feature of a goal is that it is temporal, which means that it is bound by time. *If the objective is not required to be accomplished by a certain date, it is not a goal. It is merely a statement or suggestion about what you may do at some point in the future.* Because goals are accompanied by a date when they must be completed, it's easy for us to group them according to similar completion dates. We typically have short-term goals, which generally represent objectives that we want to accomplish within the next five years. We also have mid-term goals, which generally represent the objectives we want to accomplish in a 10-year period after the short-term goals have been reached. And finally, we have long-term goals, which are the objectives that we want to accomplish within a 15-year period after the mid-term goals have been reached. Goals should therefore represent the objectives that you want to accomplish over a 30-year period,[xiv] i.e., a time period that is long enough to make leaving a legacy realistic, achievable and worthy of thinking about and working on right now.

Goal-setting takes time and often requires both reflection and introspection. As you formulate your goals you should use a process called *compounding or positive reinforcement,* in which your short-term goals, help you to achieve your mid-term goals, which in turn help you to achieve your long-term goals.

> *It is not enough to take a step which may someday lead to a goal; each step must be itself a goal and a step likewise.*
>
> — *Johan Wolfgang von Goethe*

ARE YOUR GOALS SMART?

In addition to compounding, your goals should also be SMART. SMART is an acronym for five important characteristics that should encompass your goals. *SMART goals are Specific, Measurable, Accountable, Relevant, and Time Bound.* Specific means that it is clearly defined. Many people have a goal of taking a dream vacation, which is great, but the dream should be more specific. A dream vacation could be to Cairo, in Egypt or to the Serengeti, in northern Tanzania or it could be to Versailles, in France. When you consider your dream vacation, you may think of Hawaii. But this isn't very specific. Hawaii is a state that encompasses many different islands. It is unclear if you want to visit the entire state or just parts of it, and if so, which parts? Which cities, which sites, which beaches or islands do you want to visit? Where do you want to stay and for how long?

✔ It is important to be **Specific.** You should describe the characteristics of the vacation. Do you want to go to Maui, or the Big Island? Do you want to see Kilauea? Do you want to go to a luau? Do you want to travel via cruise ship, airline, private charter? What time of year will you go? Who do you want to go with you? You must be specific because it helps you (1) determine the cost of the trip, (2) have a detailed plan to follow before and during your trip, and (3) understand the overall impact it will have on your legacy.

✓ Goals should also be **Measurable**. This allows you to track your progress relative to your goal. If you're behind schedule, you can work to catch up and if you're off track, you can take counter-measures to get back on track. Measurable means that you should be able to quantify it. And if they're already specific, it's much easier to quantify and measure them.

✓ Your goals should also allow for **Accountability**. It's always a good idea to have someone in your corner who can help hold you accountable. While you can try to reach your goals alone, it is often much easier if you have someone who cares about you to encourage you. It is helpful to have a supporter and an advocate, who checks in and asks, "How are you doing? Are you almost there? Do you need help?" He or she can also encourage you during tough times, especially when you don't know if you can keep going. But be careful because not everyone who thinks they are holding you accountable is actually doing so. Sometimes they are just being critical, saying things like, "I knew you were never going take that trip," or, "I told you it was a bad idea." That's not holding you accountable. That's being disparaging and you don't want those kind of toxic personalities as part of your accountability team.

✓ Goals should also be **Relevant.** Goals should reinforce and strengthen other goals and they should be consistent with stewardship, owner-ship, and legacy. A dream vacation might also be one that's experiential and transformative. You may want to visit Ghana to see the slave castles and the "door of no return," where our ancestors where forced through before being taken to the New World. You may want to visit Israel to see the Holy Land. Or you may want to go to Lalibela, in Ethiopia, where Saint Lalibela attempted to build a new Jerusalem, where 12 churches were carved out of a single piece of stone. It is considered one of the great wonders of the world. These kinds of vacations help you and your children to see new things, to learn, to grow, to understand and appreciate their heri-tage and current blessings.

✓Each goal must also be **Time Bound**. There is nothing like a deadline to focus the mind. I'm sure you are familiar with Steve Jobs who co-founded Apple Inc. People who worked with him said he had something called the reality distortion field. Jobs would often ask his engineering team to build a new feature or redesign an existing feature for him within a week. They would respond that they could get it done in six weeks if they *really* pushed it. Jobs would then say, "I don't think you heard me. I need it next week." Sure enough, they would figure out how to build and deliver it to him in a week. I'm sure that we've all completed an assignment, a project, or a deliverable in a week that normally would have taken three weeks. We finished it because it had to be done by a certain time. This is why deadlines are vital—*they focus the mind* and help us accomplish tasks.

With that framework in mind you should be in a great position to lay out your short, medium, and long-term goals, while ensuring that they are SMART, compounding, and consistent with stewardship, ownership, and legacy.

LAY THE RIGHT FOUNDATION BEFORE YOU SKIP AHEAD

Now, you might be thinking, "Look, I really like this high-level goal setting thing, but please cut to the chase and tell me exactly what I need to do to retire comfortably." Okay, since you're twisting my arm, I'll go right into it. If we look at the median income for the average American household, it's about $56,000 per year, but for our purposes let's use $50,000 per year. It is a nice round number that makes the calculations easier. So, if your household has a $50,000 annual income, how much money would you need to retire and maintain your current level of spending?

The answer is that you'd need about 20 times your current income, which, in this case, is $1 million. That's how much money you need to have invested at retirement and generating an average return of 5% each year. Why $1 million and why a 5% return? Most financial analysts assume that the market will grow at 5% per year over the very long term. They assume this because that's about what the market has done since people started tracking it. So, if you had $100 invested in the market you should on average expect to have $105 the next year[xv]. The $5 increase is equivalent to a 5% return on the initial $100 investment. Therefore, if you had $1,000,000 invested in the market and generating a 5% return, you could expect to have $1,050,000 at the end of the next year. In that case, a 5% return would lead to a $50,000 increase and that's the amount you would live on each year.

So how much would you need to put away every year for the next 40 years, earning a 5% return, to have a million dollars? That would require about $8,000 a year or $667 a month or 16% of your salary. That's a lot, right? Now you might be a saver, but 16% is a lot to save a month. Maybe you can't realistically save 16% of your salary but let's suppose that you are able to commit to 10%. That percentage today is huge and means you can invest $5,000 a year or $417 a month. That's great, but you still have a gap of $3,000 a year, or $250 a month, to close. So, how do we close that gap?

MAXIMIZE EVERY TOOL AND BENEFIT AT YOUR DISPOSAL

Let's start with something called a 401k plan, which is basically a long-term, tax-deferred, investment plan offered by many employers to help their employees save for retirement. If you put a portion of your salary into a 401k plan, the government will not require you to pay taxes on that money until you take it out in the future. If you take it out after age 59 1/2, you will pay taxes at that point. If you take it out *before* age 59 1/2, you're going to pay the taxes you owe *plus a penalty*. If you put money in your 401k and you leave it in there, even though the money may be earning a return each year, the government will not tax you on that return until you take it out. Got it?

About 80% of companies have some kind of 401k plan, so chances are that yours also has one. Most of these companies will match some portion of the money you put in. So, your company may also contribute $0.25, $0.50, or even $1 for each dollar you put in. The average match in the United States is about 4% of your salary. If you put the $5,000 that you are saving into a 401k plan sponsored by your company, and the company matches your contribution up to 4%, that would give you another $2,000 per year from your employer. *That's free money. That's why you should try your best to get any and all matching contributions provided by your employer. There is no investment that gives you a return like that.* That's a 100% return if your company is matching your contribution dollar for dollar. You put in a dollar, they put in a dollar. I like that return. You should like it too, and ensure that you never leave any matching funds on the table.

Now you've got $7,000 of the $8,000 that you need, but remember that the $5,000 you put in is not being taxed until you take it out because the government is trying to encourage you to save for retirement. That means that you get tax benefits *now*. Instead of paying taxes on a taxable income of $50,000, you would only pay taxes on taxable income of $45,000[xvi]. If your tax rate was 25% then you would save $1,250[xvii] in taxes and you can invest those savings. Now you have $8,250[xviii] and you are well on your way to having $1,000,000 at retirement. In this situation, what you have done, is turn your $5,000 annual investment into an $8,250 investment every single year, which puts you in position to leave a huge legacy for your children's children. But if you don't invest the $5,000, you not only lose an opportunity to be a millionaire when you retire, you also lose an opportunity to leave a million-dollar inheritance to your children and their children.

Investing a portion of your salary annually for 40 years sounds like a huge leap but it is extremely important. While not everyone has 40 years ahead of them, many young people do. In the 2014–2015 school year, close to 4 million[xix] students graduated from college. One million graduated with associate's degrees, 2 million with bachelor's degrees, 800,000 with master's degrees, and 170,000 with doctoral degrees. Of those students, 430,000 were African-American and 285,000 were Latino. Almost all of these young people have 40 years ahead of them and the vast majority of them will likely work for companies that have 401k plans. *Yet each one of these students may be about to make a million-dollar mistake if they are not aggressively saving and investing a portion of their salary.* That adds up to $4 trillion in retirement funds, that are at risk across the total group of graduates. And of that $4 trillion, $430 billion is at risk for the African-American students and $285 billion is at risk for Latino students.

This is a massive problem. Why? Because (1) the average American couple only has $5,000 saved for retirement[xx] but needs close to $1 million, (2) 43% of working-age families have no retirement savings at all, and (3) only 8% of African-Americans and 4% of Latino senior households are economically secure[xxi]. These are terrifying statistics, especially for African-American and Latino seniors who will likely have to keep working for as long as they can.

TAX BENEFITS FOR INDEPENDENT CONTRACTORS

If you are one of the millions of independent consultants in the US workforce who are not employees of a corporation and therefore do not get any matching funds, you might be wondering what you can do. While you may not receive matching contributions, you're still eligible to participate in tax-deferred retirement plans that provide you with important tax benefits that are similar to the employer sponsored 401k plan. *These tax benefits will allow your contributions to (1) lower your current taxable income and (2) grow tax-free until you are eligible to withdraw the funds penalty-free in the future.* Instead of a traditional company sponsored 401k plan, entrepreneurs and independent consultants can set up and contribute to one of several retirement plans which include; (1) the one participant IRA (Solo IRA) for self-employed individuals or business owners with no employees other than a spouse, (2) the Simplified Employee Pension IRA (SEP IRA) for self-employed individuals or business owners including those with employees, and (3) the Savings Incentive Match Plan for Employees IRA (SIMPLE IRA) for self-employed individuals and businesses with 100 or fewer employees.

While the plan you choose will ultimately depend on your circumstances—if you have employees, if you are a sole proprietor, if there are multiple owners and/or shareholders, if your revenues are modest or robust—some of these plans could allow the total annual contribution made to your retirement to be *tens of thousands more* than what could be otherwise made in a company sponsored 401k plan. This means that as your entrepreneurial or consulting income rises, the total amount of tax-deferred contributions made to your retirement could easily make up for, and in some cases greatly surpass, the impact of the average matching contributions from a company sponsored 401k plan.

Let's look at the numbers. If you made $100,000 a year at a company with a 401k plan and you contributed $18,000 (the max allowed per year by the IRS) to your 401k plan, with the company contributing a 100% (dollar for dollar) match for all of your contributions up to 6% of your salary (i.e., $6,000), you would have an additional $24,000 ($18,000 plus $6,000) added to your 401k plan that year. Two of the benefits of the company sponsored plan include (1) $4,500 of tax savings and, of course, (2) $6,000 of company match. If you are self-employed with a Solo IRA plan and earned $100,000 after the requisite expenses, you could contribute $18,000 to your Solo IRA and your business could also contribute up to 25% of your self-employment earnings, which would be $25,000. In this scenario, the total amount added to your retirement earnings would be $43,000, which is almost $20,000 more than the company-sponsored 401k and could equate to $1,300,000 more in retirement assets for the entrepreneur. As you can see, the potential is great for independent contractors, consultants, and entrepreneurs who keep their knowledge of financial matters high, their expenses low, and their cash flow high.

Let's say you earned less than $100,000 (somewhere between $35,000 and $50,000). After expenses, you could contribute as much as you can to your Solo IRA (perhaps $2,500 to $5,000) and increase it over time as your business grows until you reach the IRS maximum (currently $18,000). At that point, you could have your business start to make contributions to your Solo IRA (up to 25% of your self-employment earning) in addition to what you are already contributing.

As a community, it is vital that our children, our relatives, and especially our seniors are aware of, and are taking advantage of, all opportunities that can help them plan for the future to retire comfortably and leave a legacy. For many people who are currently in the workforce as employees or independent contractors or consultants, and the students who are graduating each year, it's not

Wealthy people don't spend principal.
Wealthy people make principal work
for them. Rich people spend principal
and that is why they go broke."

always that opportunities aren't available to them. Quite often it's that they don't *know what they should do with those opportunities* so they can accumulate the income generating resources they need in retirement.

ARE YOU TRYING TO BECOME RICH, OR WEALTHY?

What I am talking about is *wealth—accumulating a million dollars of income generating assets at retirement.* In my example, I didn't talk about spending the million dollars during retirement. I discussed using the returns generated by that million dollars to maintain your current level of spending during retirement. That's what wealth does. Wealthy people don't spend principal. Wealthy people make principal work for them. Rich people spend principal and that is why they go broke. Remember the lottery winners, professional athletes, and entertainers we talked about? I know a few young ladies with trust funds. These young ladies have what some people might call "real money." But you know what they spend? Yep, you guessed it, they spend a portion of what their principal generates. That's it.

Most people would look at their assets and say, "Wow, I've got a lot of money. I can spend a lot of it and still be rich." But what wealthy people see is the $50,000 a year that the million generates. That's it. From their perspective that's all they have. And, if their investment generates, $47,000 one year, that's what they're going to spend. If on the other hand, it generates $53,000, they're going to spend $50,000 and add the $3,000 back to the principal, which is going to drive even more returns in the future. They have a completely different mindset and all things being equal, as long as they don't touch the principal, they'll have money for the rest of their lives.

But for many of us, the problem and the challenge is that we don't have the right mindset or the necessary information. Despite having very limited resources, it's easy to find ways to spend money on things we don't truly need, because we live in a society that rewards appearance over substance. That's why we must be careful about focusing on superficial things like what people wear, where they live, or what they drive. Looks can be deceiving because many folks struggle with financial insecurity and try to give the impression that they are doing better than they really are. If someone drives up in an expensive car or a flashy sports car, we're going to assume that they are doing well. But the truth is that they could be paying $1,200 a day for an expensive rental car or be up to their necks in high interest rate credit card debt. Remember, you don't know what people *own*, you only see what they possess and *possession does not mean ownership.*

WHAT ABOUT COLLEGE SAVINGS, A DOWN PAYMENT ON A HOME, AND EMERGENCY FUNDS?

By now, you probably have a handle on saving for retirement and legacy, but there are other things that you may need to do. You've got college funds to think about. You have a down payment on a home to come up with. You may need an emergency fund.

Let's start with higher education, which is an excellent path to wealth building. How much should you save for college? The short answer is that to cover 100% of the "out of pocket" cost for a private four-year university you'll need to save and invest $10,000 a year or $833 a month for 18 years per child to cover the cost of college. That's $290,000 per child (or $73,000 per year per child) for a top tier private four-year university. *With a mindset focused on stewardship, ownership, and legacy, your goal should be focused on getting your child the highest possible education at the lowest possible cost.* A cost that includes no debt whatsoever. That should be the goal. I've often said that excellence gets funded while mediocracy gets the privilege of borrowing. In most circumstances a 3.9 GPA will sell itself, and attract a lot of funding, but a 1.6 GPA will always be a tough sell and won't attract any funding without an extraordinarily compelling story to complement it. So, your children's job should be

(1) to deliver academic excellence, first and foremost, which can then be bolstered with community service, athletics, and other forms of well roundedness and (2) to strategically and passionately shop that excellence to numerous local, state, regional, and national scholarship providing entities.

You can also easily save $120,000 to $160,000 per child by sending your child to an excellent four-year, in-state public university (like Penn State, North Carolina A&T, FAMU, Ohio State, University of Michigan, SUNY,

> "You need to have a plan to be able to comfortably make the down payment no matter how much it is or how great your credit score"

or UConn to name only a few) vs. sending them to a typical private four-year university. You can save another $44,000 if your child does her first two years of college at a local community college and then transfers to an excellent four year in-state public university for the last two years. You can save an additional $60,000 to $80,000 if your child can secure $15,000 to $20,000 of outside scholarships each year.

If your child has strong academic performance, this target is very attainable because, in many cases, he or she can easily secure $5,000 in scholarships per year from your church, local companies, and various community organizations. If you are a "low-income family" there are over 35 first-tier private universities that will waive tuition, and in some cases also cover room and board, if your child is accepted. Military academies, the Coast Guard academy, ROTC, and the G.I. Bill will also cover most, if not all, of the costs of his or her college education. One of my mentees went to UConn with a full scholarship and graduated top of her class (in four years she got all A's and one A minus) with no debt. This means that after college she got to keep the maximum amount of her income versus allocating thousands of dollars to repaying student loans, like many of her peers.

If you are intent on having your child go to a private four-year university, you should ensure that the cost to do so is no more than the lowest cost alternative. Since the *cost of a college education is astronomically high, trying to fund it with your own cash, supplemented by debt, should be your last resort.* That way, you can reallocate the money you saved for college to help your child start a business, fund graduate school, buy a home, or spend a year in a Third World country starting a school, helping farmers, or developing small businesses.

How much should you save for a down payment on a new home? That depends on the characteristics of the home and the location. If we talk about the average price in the US, it's about $250,000. If we're talking about Manhattan, you have to be over $3 million to enter the luxury market. If you are looking at a home that costs around $250,000, and you're putting about 20% down, you need to have $50,000. To accumulate $50,000 you must save and invest $4,500 a year, or $375 a month, for 15 years. There are programs that don't require 20% down, but you never know what the economy is going to be like when you're ready to buy a home. We bought our home after the economic downturn, and while we got a great deal on the price, the banks at that time weren't lending to anyone in our area with less than 20% down, even with a stellar credit score, which we had. So, you need to have a plan to be able to comfortably make the down payment no matter how much it is or how great your credit score.

How much should you put away to have a fully-funded emergency account or rainy-day fund? Before I answer that question, it important to know that 62% of Americans have no emergency savings at all[xxii]. Yes, you read that correctly, *no emergency savings at all*. Now, a general rule is that you should have about six to 12 months of after-tax salary for a rainy-day fund. The amount of the fund should be based on your specific set of circumstances, which includes the length of time it takes for you, or people in your field or industry, to find a new job. For some people, whose skills are in high demand and whose network is strong, it can take less than a month to get a new job. For others, it might take 18 months to find a new job. With a $50,000 salary, you'd have to put away $6,000 a year, or $500 a month, for five years to have 12 months of after-tax salary on hand for emergencies. That's a lot of money.

WHY LEGACY IS SO IMPORTANT

Another set of important costs that we haven't discussed is the start-up costs our children face when they leave home. These costs can easily be $10,000 to $15,000, which includes their first month's rent, last month's rent, security deposit, new furniture, or a down payment on a car. For most of us, it's very hard to save enough money to fund all of these expenses while also paying our monthly bills. Therefore, you can see the power and importance of being able to leave a legacy for your children's children. Can you imagine the economic freedom you'd have starting out if the start-up costs for your first apartment were already funded? Or if the down payment on your first home, your emergency funds, or your college funds were already covered? That would make a huge difference for a lot of households. Can you imagine if you could look forward to an inheritance like that, and the impact it would have on your ability to fund your retirement and leave a legacy? Sadly, in most cases, an inheritance is an advantage most of us simply don't have. This makes it incredibly difficult to accumulate wealth because we're often starting from scratch and funding everything at the same time.

> " A few years ago, a colleague of mine, I'll call him Dave, told me about an inheritance he received when his parents passed away. It was about $500,000, which would seem like a lot of money to many people, but not to him. He appreciated it, but it was split among two other siblings. They each got $167,000 incremental cash that they didn't have to pay tax on. To Dave, it wasn't that big of a deal; it helped, but it wasn't like he could stop working. That's a whole different level of reality. Can you imagine what $167,000 would do for your retirement, emergency fund, mortgage, or for your ability to leave an inheritance for your children and their children?
>
> That's why we focus on stewardship, ownership, and legacy. Because despite our current disadvantages, we are going to do all that we can to ensure that our children don't inherit the same situation we did. I'll be honest with you, I did not have those advantages when I was starting out. In fact, our family situation is such that when somebody dies, we don't get an inheritance, we get a bill. "

It's important to remember that *legacy starts with stewardship and stewardship starts with understanding your current situation*. While we covered a lot in that last discussion, the key takeaway is that if you skip ahead without ensuring that the right foundation is in place, it can be overwhelming and might reduce your resolve to accomplish your goals. So, let's get back to the basics and focus on ensuring that the fundamentals are in place before we address more advanced concerns. I want you to visualize a map that has several flags on it that represent important destinations. For you to get to any of these destinations, you must understand your current position. *From a financial perspective, if you don't know your current cash flow position, in clear and well-defined terms, you won't be able to navigate a path to get to your ultimate goal.*

IT'S NOT WHAT YOU MAKE, IT'S WHAT YOU KEEP

The first step to achieving your financial goals is to understand your current household cash flow position. As you seek to determine that position, it's important to understand that *stewardship is not just how much you make, it's more about how much you keep*. While it may be hard to imagine, there are many lower income households that have higher levels of cash flow than higher income households. How does this happen? Imagine a household that makes $50,000 a year. They have debt, they're paying taxes, and they have household expenses (some essential and some non-essential). After those expenses are paid, let's say they have about $437 a month of cash flow left (or about 10% of their income). Now, think about a household that makes 50% more income, or $75,000 a year, but has much less cash flow (perhaps only $187 per month, or just 3% of their income). How is that possible? It's because the higher income family has a different cost structure with different priorities and different spending habits. The challenge is that as income increases, expenses also tend to increase. When a family's annual income grows, say from $50,000 to $75,000, they may upgrade their car, their neighborhood, and their wardrobe. All of these additional expenses will be funded by the increase in their annual salary. *That's why as our income goes up our cash flow doesn't always increase proportionally.*

In a previous career, I would travel all over the world meeting entrepreneurs and buying various companies. To ascertain how successful a company was performing and its valuation, I would look at a lot of factors, but one of the most important factors was the company's operating income as a percentage of their sales. This is called a Return on Sales (ROS)[xxiii] or EBIT [xxiv] margin.

ROS tells you a lot about how a person or team runs a company and I would much rather buy a company that was making $30 million a year in sales with a 10% ROS (i.e., $3 million of profit before tax) than a company that was making $100 million a year with a 3% ROS ($3 million of profit before tax). A low ROS means that the return on all your effort is not very impressive and says something about how you run your business or the attractiveness of the industry that you've chosen, neither of which is good. While the amount of money you earn annually might seem impressive, it doesn't tell the

"If you fail to plan, you're planning to fail."
What is truly remarkable about his quote
is that you cannot escape planning. "

whole story. Maybe you're doing well, or maybe you're not. The real question is how much cash flow do you have left after your expenses are paid? At the end of the day, *it's the bottom line that tells the real story and we rarely ever get to see other people's bottom line.*

Not only do we not get to see people's bottom line, we are also trained to value superficial things in life. Think about it, the average American watches five-

and-a-half hours of TV per day and the average African-American watches close to six-and-a-half hours of TV a day. You simply cannot watch that much media and not be influenced by almost $200 billion of advertising. There are even songs with the lyrics, "We don't even look at the price tag," as if that is something to be proud of. If you sell luxury goods, you couldn't hope for a better customer than someone who does not look at the price tag. In addition to that, many people across various forms of media regularly talk about how much they make and the luxury items they like to buy, which helps to normalize superficial lifestyles. Very few of these folks talk about stewardship, ownership, or legacy or how they manage to keep the maximum amount of their hard-earned money. That is, if they do manage to keep it.

Don't get me wrong, there is nothing wrong with a desire to have high-quality goods. I tend to wear designer suits, but I also work hard to stay in line with stewardship principles. While my suits are designer, most of them are bought at 70–80% off because I purchase well-made items at discount prices. I never compromise quality and I never will. *Price is what you pay, value is what you get, and I always insist on value at a low price.* It is important that we never assume that someone is doing well because they're looking good. We don't really know what their situation is. We may see people who *drive* nice cars, but do they *own* those cars? Very often they don't. Cars are big-ticket items and it's expensive to own a car outright, so most people have to borrow the money to buy a car. Think about someone who's making large payments on a luxury car versus someone who owns a non-luxury car. Who do we praise? Who do we value more? Who do we celebrate and want to emulate? Nine times out of 10, it's the person in the expensive car. Because of this skewed perception, we're constantly making value judgments that take us down the wrong path.

At the end of the day, it's about how much cash flow you have and where it's going. Is it establishing ownership and building your legacy? Or are you merely funding someone else's legacy?

YOU NEED A FULLY BURDENED BUDGET

If you want to establish ownership and fund your legacy, you're going to need a fully burdened budget. You might be thinking, "What is this 'fully burdened budget' business you're talking about? I'm not so sure I'm feeling you on this whole budget thing. I really like the scripture part, so how about you throw in some more scriptures."

Look, I hear you. Budgets are *not* sexy. The kind of budget I'm talking about is definitely not sexy. But here's the thing. I used to work in the corporate sector and for those of you who are working in the corporate sector now, your livelihood is based on a budget. I know because I used to create and review those corporate budgets, and I can tell you that you don't get paid unless you're on that budget—a budget that's been through months of development and reviewed at every level. Every benefit that you get, every salary increase you get or don't get, the very position you currently have, the building that you're in, the team you are a part of, is on somebody's budget. It's vitally important. It has been developed, reviewed, and approved every year without fail. If not, it would be malpractice and bad business. People would be fired immediately. Stock prices would plummet. Budgets are not sexy but they're necessary for financial survival, for excellence, and for funding your legacy. But do we have our own personal budgets or our own household budgets? If it is malpractice for corporations that are worth trillions of dollars to not have a budget, then it is certainly malpractice for us to not have one. We need to have one, our kids need to have one, and they've got to understand it and be familiar and conversant with it.

Planning is vital. As a matter of fact, it's so vital that corporations call their budgeting process "planning."

The whole organization is called Finance and Planning, which just means finance and budgets. Ben Franklin famously said, "If you fail to plan, you're planning to fail." What is truly remarkable about his quote is that you *cannot escape planning*. Either you have a plan to get to a destination or goal that has some benefit for you and your family, or you are planning to fail. You are planning one way or the other. You cannot escape it, so if you don't have a plan, you've already lost. Since you were asking about scripture and trying to get away from the whole budget thing, what does the Bible say about plans and planning?

The plans of the diligent lead to profit
as surely as haste leads to poverty.
— *Proverbs 21:5*

Plans are established by seeking advice;
so, if you wage war, obtain advice.
— *Proverbs 20:18*

Plans fail for lack of counsel but with
many advisers they succeed.
— *Proverbs 15:22*

The plans of the diligent lead to profit. Diligence is about being careful, persistent, and consistent. Diligence is not something you do some days or sometimes, but *all* the time. Even secular companies employ these proverbs from thousands of years ago and you should, too. Since plans are established by seeking advice, the question is who do you consult when you're making important decisions? And since a leader is only as effective as the wise counsel around him or her—who is your wise counsel?

Clearly, financial plans are important and a budget is a vital part of your plan. But we're not talking about a typical budget, we're talking about a *fully burdened budget*. You're probably wondering what a fully burdened budget is. To get to that answer, let's consider your budget. I'm sure that you're well aware of what your mortgage or rent is, as well as your car payment, your cell phone bill, and insurance payments. We all know those expenses because if we ever forget to pay those bills, our creditors will happily remind us who really owns the house or the car. So, there's no doubt that you know how much you're spending on those items, because those are what I call *known expenses. Known expenses are generally easy to understand because (1) you've heard about them all your life, (2) they are presented to you as a consolidated number, (3) they don't fluctuate much, and (4) you receive them on a regular and consistent basis.*

WHAT IS A PHANTOM EXPENSE?

It's not the known expenses you should be worried about, it's the other *expenses that you are committed to but don't account for* and, therefore, never show up on your budget. These items are called *phantom expenses*. They may include things like shopping, yoga, manicures and pedicures, movies, gifts, charity and so much more. Regardless of what they are, they need to be in your budget because if you're spending money on something, it has to be accounted for. Phantom expenses are a massive category that is comprised of different types of expenditures that are unique to you and your household. The unifying theme is that they don't show up on your budget and, for some people, they *can amount to as much as 20% to 25% of their total monthly spend.*

Here are some examples of phantom expenses. Family reunions are very important events for many families. If you're hosting the family reunion it can be quite expensive. Just traveling to the family reunion can be a huge expense. Whether the reunion happens once a year or once every other year, whether you're the host family or traveling to the host family, it must be a part of your budget. Your first thought might not necessarily be to put it in your budget but it must be in there because it may be a significant expense. If you enjoy taking dance classes, are fanatical about supporting your favorite sports team, enjoy stamp collecting or gaming or whatever it is, if you spend money on it, it needs to be in your budget.

Maybe you enjoy playing poker because it's relaxing and allows you to hang out with your friends. You play once a week, or every other week, and it costs you between $50 to $150 when you play, and can add up to around $100 to $500 a month. It needs to be in your budget. If you are on the dating scene looking for that special someone, and the process of dating includes dinners, drinks, concerts, plays, movies, meals, and entertainment, those expenses need to be in your budget. Perhaps you like to have a glass of red wine every evening to unwind and decompress. Since there are four glasses in a bottle and you have a glass a day, that's going to be five bottles per month. If you don't like lower-priced wines, because either your palate is refined or you've been influenced by the $200 billion of advertising that encourages us to want a higher priced vintage that costs say, $48 per bottle, that's going to be a $240 monthly bill that should be accounted for.

Perhaps you enjoy going to happy hour or having a beer after a hard day's work. Hey, you deserve it. You've had to put up with a lot over the course of your day and now you're trying to relax. I totally understand, but it needs to be in your budget. And by the way, since there are 365 days in a year, if you're doing anything with regularity, it's going to add up to a significant amount of money and should be in your budget. A $5 coffee and a bagel in the morning may not sound like much, but when you're buying them 365 mornings in a year they can add up, and the impact can be huge. *Remember, a phantom expense is anything that you spend money on, that you don't track, and has a cumulative negative effect on your budget.*

Now let me get back to answering your question about just what the heck is a fully burdened budget.

A fully burdened budget includes all sources of income and everything that reduces that income such as phantom expenses:

✓ **All streams of income, including salaries, rental income, child support, social security, your side hustle**

✓ **Items that reduce your income**:

- All taxes: federal, state and local income taxes, property taxes, and sales taxes

- All debt payments, including first mortgage, second mortgage, credit cards, car notes, and student loans

- All utilities, including electric, cable, Internet, mobile phone, home security, gas, and water

- All forms of insurance, including renter's insurance, homeowner's insurance, life insurance, car insurance, medical insurance, and mortgage protection insurance

- All transportation costs, including gas, roadside assistance, maintenance, car washes, and, also groceries, clothes, and food that you buy when you're traveling to and from work

- All gifts and charity and any expenses related to holidays, birthdays, weddings, tithes, offerings, and charitable giving
- All health and beauty expenses including hair care, skin care, vitamins, manicures and pedicures, massages, gym memberships, and yoga or wellness classes
- All household expenses, including, groceries, clothing, supplies, maintenance, and renovation
- All childcare and related expenses, including after school programs, summer school programs, daycare

✓ **All other expenses not included on this list**

After you've identified your phantom expenses and listed all your known expenses and subtracted them both from your income, you will have a precise view of your current household cash flow and can figure out your fully burdened budget.

To sum it up: *A fully burdened budget includes all forms of income, minus all known expenses and all phantom expenses, this equals your current household cash flow.* Your current household cash flow is a number that should be familiar to you because it might be: (1) the amount by which your bank account goes up or down on a monthly basis, (2) the amount by which your credit cards increase on a monthly basis, (3) the amount that you borrow from family and friends to stay afloat, or some combination of the three.

In any case, at the end of the day, the money has to

come from somewhere. If the cash flow from your fully burdened budget is not familiar to you, you should calculate your expenses again because there's probably a phantom expense that you did not catch – *and you must catch everything*. That way, you'll have a clear idea of what you're spending on a monthly and yearly basis.

A fully burdened budget is an essential part of stewardship because it forces you to identify every expense and shows you the amount of cash flow you have available for maximizing ownership (eliminating debt) and leaving a legacy (retiring with dignity, leaving an inheritance and seeding into those in need). People often talk about where they want to be in the future, which is a wonderful thing, but they don't know precisely where they are now, or what they have to work with. That makes it very difficult for them to develop an effective plan to achieve their goals. The first step is always understanding your current household cash flow because achieving your goals requires cash flow and you need to know if you have enough to fund the journey.

Luke 14:28 says, "For which of you intending to build a tower does not sit down first and count the cost." Counting the cost means, how much capital will you need? From what source? In what time? At what cost? Consider how the Temple in Jerusalem was built.

David created detailed plans and raised an enormous amount of money to finance the construction. He also set the example by using his own money (the equivalent of billions in today's dollars) and asked his subjects to follow suit. We must ensure that we are doing the same things, otherwise, "lest after he has laid the foundation and cannot finish, all who see him will mock him." How we manage our resources today, has a direct impact on the legacy that we will leave behind and what we're going to receive in the hereafter. *If you want those "crowns" in the afterlife, you need to handle the "crowns" in this life.*

CHAPTER 4

Maximizing Your Household Cash Flow

REDUCING EXPENSES IS EASIER THAN INCREASING INCOME

You've learned about the goal setting process, identified your phantom expenses, developed a fully burdened budget, and determined your current cash flow. The next step is to maximize your household cash flow by taking actions that help you reduce your expenses in a reasonable, sustainable, and consistent way. Why is the focus on reducing expenses and not increasing revenue or earning? (1) If you could have easily increased your salary, you would have already done so, (2) increasing salary takes time and often requires upfront and ongoing investment, and (3) reducing ex-

penses has always had a far bigger and more immediate impact on cash flow than increasing revenue.

When the average company reduces expenses, up
to 83%[xxv] of every dollar saved falls to the bottom line.
However, when the same company increases revenue, only about 7.5%[xxvi] of every dollar earned falls to
the bottom line (since they have to pay taxes and sub-
tract all the costs required to generate that revenue).
Therefore, *$1 of cost reductions can have 11 times
more impact on the bottom line than $1 of incremen-
tal revenue.* This is why companies are always looking
at cost reductions and have so many names for it; off
shoring, right sizing, attrition, voluntary retirements,
separations, terminations, layoffs, and cost down, to
name a few. While a corporation's goal is always to
increase profits, your goal must always be to increase
stewardship, ownership, and legacy. When a household with a legacy mindset reduces its expense by $1,
100% of that dollar goes to funding their ownership
and legacy. *When a household without a legacy mindset saves an extra $1, 100% of it typically goes to fund-
ing someone else's ownership and legacy.*

So, is it possible to take action that can increase
your cash flow by another $200, $300, or perhaps
even $1,500 per month? The answer is yes. Let's find
out how.

KNOW THYSELF AND UNDERSTAND YOUR NEGATIVE MULTIPLIERS

The first thing you're going to do is take out the axe and cut all expenses by 20%. Everything gets cut. Done. End of story and we live happily ever after. That doesn't sound very realistic, does it? That's because it's not. Cutting everything would be a foolish thing to do. The first thing you must do before you start reducing any expense is to examine yourself and your lifestyle. "Know thyself" is an ancient African proverb, known the world over. It means that to *fully understand what is going on around you, you must first understand what is going on inside of you.* The current relationship that we have with money and finances is formed in our childhood and is ingrained in us to such an extent that we are not even aware of why we handle our finances the way we do. Before you make any changes, there are several questions you should first ask yourself:

1. **When you were growing up, did you feel like you were deprived of important material possessions or emotional support?**
   - Why did you feel that way?
   - Where you teased about having a lack of possessions?

2. **Are there certain purchases that make you feel secure, valued, or loved?**
   - If so, how frequently do you make these purchases?
   - What emotional triggers lead to these purchases?

3. **Did you grow up with friends who had possessions that you desired but could not afford?**

- How did that make you feel?
- What did you do in response to that feeling?

4. **Did you grow up with an abundance of material possessions?**
   - Did you regularly receive the things that you desired most?
   - Were you given gifts or presents in place of love or emotional support?

5. **Did you grow up feeling insecure about your appearance?**
   - Do you still feel that way now?
   - How have you compensated for that feeling of insecurity?

6. **What was your parents', guardians', or mentor's philosophy about money and spending?**
   - What is your philosophy about money and spending?
   - Are your actions consistent with your philosophy?

It's important to understand the extent to which past experiences affect your current motives, values, and insecurities with respect to money and spending. Regardless of whether you're single or in a committed relationship, it will be very difficult to change your spending and savings patterns if you don't understand the behavior or thought process behind them. Before you do anything else, take some time to answer these questions and reflect on your answers. It will pay huge dividends going forward and make it much easier for you to stay the course.

It is also imperative that you identify expenses that have a negative multiplier effect. *Negative multipliers are expenses that have an impact that far outweighs the amount saved by reducing or eliminating it.* An item that has a negative multiplier effect in our household is the money we spend to have our home cleaned twice a month. When we are trying to optimize our budget, that's not an item that we look to cut or significantly reduce. Why? Because, my wife's standard for cleanliness, and her expectation about what constitutes a job well done, is much higher than mine. I may put in an incredible amount of time, energy, effort, and "love" when I clean to get the portion that I'm responsible for to a standard that I think is amazing, but, unfortunately, it may not meet her standard. That leads to an opportunity for conflict because she might feel that she is not being heard or that I've not delivered, and I might feel like she's not appreciating all the hard work that I put into it. Therefore, we decided to have a service come in and clean the house for us. They can do the job in a way that's good enough for her, at a price that works for us. That allows us to focus on more important things and avoid conflict. Ultimately, it's not something that's worth cutting from our budget because the negative impact would not be worth the savings.

A friend of mine grew up in a situation where his family did not always have enough food in the house and it used to cause them a great deal of concern and anxiety. As an adult, his household always has an extra supply of food items because it gives him comfort to know that, no matter what else happens, they will never go hungry. Cutting his food budget would not be a good place to start because it could lead to more harm (and anxiety) than the "good" generated by increased savings. Why? Because the underlying issue has not been addressed.

> ❝ My wife's birthday is two days after Christmas. When she was growing up, she would get one gift for her birthday and for Christmas. Everyone else got a gift for their birthday and a separate gift for Christmas but she got one gift for both. To her, it felt like her birthday was being ignored and she never wanted to feel that way as an adult because, like everyone else, her birthday is special to her. So, trying to save money by giving her one gift for both days is not a good idea and would certainly have a negative multiplier effect."

While negative multipliers are unique to each individual, couple, or household, it's important that you identify them so you can clearly see the items that should be taken off the table.

Increasing your cash flow requires incredible restraint and can be challenging because it requires you to keep your spending under control. That's why I encourage you to set aside a certain amount of money, on a weekly basis, that is available for you and your partner to spend however you please. This should be done after you've maximized your cash flow, so you know how much you have to fund it. It should be an amount that is reasonable, perhaps $20 to $50 a week, depending on your circumstances. Spend it on whatever you want without asking for permission or getting approval. As long as you keep it under the budgeted amount and it's not used in a nefarious way, it will help you to relieve stress and keep your sanity.

At this point you have your budget, *it's fully burdened*, and everything's in there. You've gone through it two or three times adding known expenses and all your *phantom expenses*. You also now understand the impact that your childhood has on your relationship with money and you've identified the *negative multipliers* that are going to be taken off the table as deductions. Now you're ready to determine the best ways to increase your cash flow.

HOW CAN I OPTIMIZE THIS?

The first step is to look at each line item in your budget and ask yourself, "How can I optimize this?" Typically, your first and largest bill is your tax bill, so let's start there. *The first rule with taxes, is to ensure that you are paying what you owe and not a penny more.* If you are a low to moderate income earner, be sure to claim the full amount of your Earned Income Tax Credit (EITC). In 2009, the EITC distributed $58 billion in refundable credits to nearly 27 million working people of low to moderate income. Researchers at Carnegie Mellon University, estimated that seven million Americans (or 25% of eligible tax payers) each failed to claim an average of $1,100[xxvii] per year of refundable tax credits. That's $11,000 per person over a 10-year period. That's a significant amount of resources that many families can't afford to lose. Forty-eight percent[xxviii] of African-American tax payers are eligible for the EITC. If you are one of them, it's important to ensure that you claim every dollar of the EITC.

To the extent that you are a household that itemizes your tax deductions, be sure to include all your charitable deductions. You may be able to increase them by donating clothes, furniture, and other items that you don't need but are still in a good condition. You'll get the added benefit of helping someone else who needs it while setting a positive example for your children, plus the financial benefit of an additional tax deduction.

If you are a senior and own a home, there are several states that will give you a tax break on your property taxes. For example, senior citizens in Florida who qualify can get a tax exemption up to $50,000[xxix] on the assessed value of their home. In New York State, seniors who qualify can receive up to a 50%[xxx] exemption on the assessed value of their home. So, while there are benefits available, you'll never get them if you don't find out if you are eligible and apply.

If you are taking care of your parents or spending money on work-related child care, you may be eligible for the Child and Dependent Care Tax Credit, which can save your household up to $2,000[xxxi] per year.

You may also want to sign up for a Flexible Spending Account (FSA) if your employer offers it. It allows you to set aside up to $2,550 per year, on a pre-tax basis, for you family's health-care costs. This could help you to save another $640[xxxii] per year in taxes. Your biggest expense can easily be your tax bill and you must ensure that you're maximizing the tax benefits available to you.

Since we live in a high consumption society, that's driven by consumer debt with remarkably high interest rates, you should also take a careful look at your debts, especially your credit cards. Not many people consider this but if you're in good standing with your credit card company you can ask them to lower your rate. Think about it, if you're faithfully paying a 30% Annual Percentage Rate (APR) why would *they voluntarily drop your rate?* They may also have a program or a customer retention initiative that will lower your rate, but you'll never know if you don't ask. The worst thing they can do is say no. There may also be an opportunity to transfer your credit debt from high-rate credit cards to low-rate cards. Balance transfers are good ways to reduce your cost and accelerate your ability to pay down the principal. One of the most important aspects of reducing your debt is *to commit to not adding any new debt* so that the maximum amount of your payment reduces your principal. In Chapter 5, I give you several ways to eliminate all of your household debt.

Another great way you and your family can save money is to buy at discount stores.

❝ One of my favorite discount stores sells excess inventory from major fashion brands. Many years ago, I graduated from business school and was stocking up on suits to start my corporate career. I went to a department store and bought several designer suits and had them tailored to fit. A couple of years later, I walked into a local discount store, glanced across the room, and saw something in the men's section that looked vaguely familiar. As I walked closer I saw one of the suits that I had bought at a department store for $700, being sold for $169, and that wasn't even the clearance price. It was a powerful (and painful) lesson. Another 10 years would pass before I purchased another suit from a department store because I shifted my shopping to discount stores. These stores allow you to *get a great deal, without having to sacrifice quality.*

Our children are still very young. Because we have a boy and a girl, our youngest can't wear the clothes that the oldest has grown out of. They also quickly grow out of the clothes we purchase for them. To save money, we buy their clothes from discount stores, secondhand stores, and consignment shops. You'd be surprised at what some people give away. We've found amazing deals on designer boots, winter coats, suits, and many necessary items. If the clothes are still in good condition when the kids grow out of them, we donate them to those in need. This allows us to teach our children about (1) the difference between price and value and (2) the impact that donating quality goods can have on people who are in need. This way, they get to see the full cycle — price, value, savings, and impact — which is very important. "

Big box stores that buy and sell in bulk can also help you save money. Buying in bulk can be very beneficial to your budget. Instead of buying small packets of sliced ham for breakfast and sandwiches, we'll buy and cook a large ham, like the one you might have at Thanksgiving, then we slice it, make small servings, and freeze them. Then, whenever we want ham, we just take a packet out of the freezer. It tastes amazing, lasts for months, and will save you half of what you would have spent otherwise. The process of finding deals and opportunities to save money is always the same regardless of what it is; clothes, shoes, cars, homes, apartments, lifestyle. You should always determine the *highest value you can get for the lowest possible price.*

Perhaps there is an opportunity to bundle your insurance. You may have renter's insurance and car insurance from two different companies. Insurance providers will give you a better price if you give them more business. Since you already have insurance, you may as well get the best price for the same coverage.

THE POWER OF PACKING A LUNCH

	Price	Per Week	Per Month	Per Year
Coffee	3	15	60	$720
Sandwich	3	15	60	$720
Breakfast	**6**	**30**	**120**	**$1,440**
Salad/Sandwich	7	35	140	$1,680
Soda	2	10	40	$480
Lunch	**9**	**45**	**180**	**$2,160**
Total	**$15**	**$75**	**$300**	**$3,600**

The table above shows a powerful, yet simple, example of how you can dramatically increase your cash flow. Eating out, as I'm sure you already know, can be very expensive. Let's look at how much we might be spending on breakfast and lunch. Now, $6 for a cup of coffee and a sandwich is very reasonable and, in many cases, we might expect to pay a lot more than that. For lunch, let's say you're trying to be healthy, so you get a salad and diet soda, or something similar, and it comes to about $9. That's $15 per day and over the course of a week, it's about $75. If you look at it over the course of a month, it's $300 and over a year, well that's $3,600. By the way, this is all after-tax money, which means that you would actually have to earn about $5,000 before tax and pay 25% in taxes to have $3,750 after tax. So, if you make $50,000 a year, that's 10% of your pre-tax salary, just on breakfast and lunch. Now, imagine what you could do with that money, if you could reclaim all or even a portion of it.

The average cost[xxxiii] of breakfast at a public school is $2.50 per day and the average cost of lunch is $2.90 per day, which combined is $5.40 every day. Since there are 180 days in a school year, the average cost for breakfast and lunch is $972 per child per year. If you have children in school and you don't qualify for the free and reduced lunch program, you can save almost $1,000 per child per year by packing a lunch for them to take to school. It's a healthy choice that can save you $12,000 per child over the course of their elementary, middle, and high school education. *If you are strapped for cash and have not started saving for college, you could easily reallocate this money to a college savings plan.*

THE POWER OF CAPTURING SMALL RAISES

# of years		1	2	3	4	5	10
Salary/Year	50,000	51,000	52,020	53,060	54,122	55,204	60,950
% Raise	2%	2%	2%	2%	2%	2%	2%
Raise (Pre-tax)/Year		1,000	1,020	1,040	1,061	1,082	1,195
Cumulative Raise		1,000	2,020	3,060	4,122	5,204	10,950
Tax (effective)	25%	25%	25%	25%	25%	25%	25%
Cumulative After-tax Incr		750	1,515	2,295	3,091	3,903	8,212
Free Cash Flow/Month		$63	$126	$191	$258	$325	$684

Here's another example. Think about the salary increases you've gotten over the course of your career. I don't know if this has happened to you, but sometimes you work really hard and your boss actually recognizes your contributions. He or she may even tell you how much the company appreciates you. Your boss may even say that, for your year-end review, you received five stars. That is certainly wonderful to hear because it's an important validation of the planning, effort, coordination, and persistence that you've shown. Perhaps your boss then tells you that to show appreciation of all the hard work you've done, your company is giving you a… drum roll please… 2% raise.

You're like… wait, what? You're stunned because you were expecting much more than 2%. Perhaps something more in line with the work that you did and also based on your stellar review. I've literally been in that situation and wondered what I was going to do with a 2% raise because I'd made financial plans based on getting a 10% raise. I was annoyed and disappointed, and wanted to say, "keep your 2%," but I didn't, even though that's how I felt. Instead I accepted the 2% increase and my plans for the 10% raise were put on hold.

After a number of years, you may begin to notice that, even though you're now making considerably more money, it still feels like you don't have more money. It's an odd feeling and you start to think back to the early part of your career and wonder what happened to those 2% raises. What does a 2% increase look like? Well, 2% of $50,000 is $1,000, but you also remember that you don't actually get the $1,000 because you have a silent partner—the federal, state, and municipal government. And you have to give a certain amount of that money to your partner. So, after taxes are taken out of the $1,000, what you actually have is $63 per month, which might make you feel like saying, "I actually went to school for this?" What is $63 per month going to do for you? But your bosses kept loving your performance and your 2% raises come in year after year.

In years one and two those 2% raises added up to $126 per month. In year five, your cumulative 2% increases added up to $325 per month. By the time you hit your tenth year, the cumulative 2% increase was almost $700, or the equivalent of a 22% pay increase over your first year. When you look back over time, you realize that *the problem wasn't the paltry 2%, the real problem is what you did with those cumulative annual $63 per month increases.* That's why you've got to capture every increase and immediately allocate it to building ownership and legacy.

THE POWER OF BASIC TAX BENEFITS

	Per Month	Per Year
Savings for Retirement	200	2,400
Day Care	800	9,600
Health Expenses	200	2,400
Retirement/Health/Dependents	**1,200**	**$14,400**

Salary (Taxable Inccome)	**$50,000**
Tax Rate	25%
Tax	**12,500**
After Tax Income	37,500
Retirement/Health/Dependents	14,400
Salary Available for Other Expenses	23,100

As I said before, one of your biggest expenses is your tax expenditure, and there may be tax benefits associated with your current spending patterns or financial situation. *It is imperative that you take advantage of every dollar of benefit that you are entitled to.*

In the table above, a person, let's call him John, is saving a small amount for retirement ($200 a month), paying for child care ($800 a month), and paying for certain health-related expenses ($200 a month). While these numbers are quite modest individually, together they add up to about $14,000 a year, which is substantial. There are four questions you should always ask yourself regarding your spending. The first is, are there any tax benefits associated with my current expenditures? The second is, do I qualify for those benefits? The third is, how much of those benefits are available to me? And the fourth is, what do I need to do to get those benefits?

If you're saving for retirement, check to see if your company has a 401k plan. As we discussed in Chapter 3, a 401k is a tax-deferred savings plan that's offered through employers to help you save for retirement. There are significant tax benefits associated with these types of plans. You can invest up to $18,000 a year in a company sponsored 401k plan and you will not be taxed on those funds until you take them out. If you take the money out before age 59 1/2, you will be taxed on the money you took out and receive an early withdrawal penalty.

In the scenario above, since John is already setting aside $200 a month, or $2,400 a year, he might as well get the tax benefit he may be entitled to. Chances are his company has a 401k plan since 80% of companies offer a 401k plan. The company may also offer an FSA

	Per Month	Per Year
401 K/IRA	200	2,400
Dependent Care Spending Account*	800	9,600
Health Care Spending Account**	200	2,400
Retirement/Health/Dependents	**1,200**	**$14,400**
* capped at 5,000/year; ** capped at 2,500/year		
Salary		**$50,000**
Retirement/Health/Dependents (Tax Deferred 2,400+5,000+2,400)		**9,800**
Taxable Income		**$40,200**
Tax Rate		25%
Tax		**10,050**
Retirement/Health/Dependents (Not Tax Deferred)		4,600
Salary Available for Other Expenses		25,550

Tax Savings	**$2,450**	**Per Year**
	$204	**Per Month**

and a dependent care spending account. These plans allow you to set aside part of your salary on a tax-free basis to pay for approved expenditures. In this case, $9,600 per year is being spent on daycare and up to $5,000 of that amount could be tax deductible. John is also spending $2,400 per year on healthcare-related expenses, all of which could also be tax deductible through a company-sponsored FSA. Since FSAs and dependent care spending accounts are "use it or lose it" programs, you have to carefully estimate your needs before putting any money in those accounts because you'll lose any amount that you don't use.

Generally, you know what your expenses are going to be for things like daycare and you can get a good sense of what you spend on health deductibles, prescriptions, and other health-related items. The end result is that $9,800 of the $14,400 of expense may actually be tax deductible. So instead of paying taxes on a taxable income of $50,000, you might now only have to pay taxes on a taxable income of $40,200. This would reduce your taxes by $2,450 per year, or $204 per month. This would significantly increase your cash flow. Again, we're talking about getting a benefit on things that you are already spending money on.

AVOID MASSIVE COSTS ON CAR PURCHASES

Let's talk about something that we are all likely to do at some point in our lives, which is buy a car. The average American who needs a car will buy about seven vehicles over the course of his or her lifetime. Most people don't have enough money to purchase a car outright so they will borrow the money to buy the car. The cost to borrow money to purchase the car is your interest rate, which can vary wildly, depending on your credit score.

	Deep Sub Prime	Sub Prime	Prime	Super Prime
Offer Price	**35,000**	**35,000**	**35,000**	**35,000**
Purchase Price	33,600	33,600	33,600	33,600
Tax, registration etc…	2,772	2,772	2,772	2,772
Down Payment	**3,000**	**3,000**	**3,000**	**7,500**
Loan	33,372	33,372	33,372	28,872
Interest Rate 2.7%, 3.6%, 10.4%, 20%	**20.00%**	**10.40%**	**3.60%**	**2.50%**
Credit Score	500 to 600	500 to 600	660 to 780	781 to 850
Term	84	84	84	84
Payment/Mo	**($741)**	**($561)**	**($450)**	**($375)**
Total Payment	($62,249)	($47,119)	($37,803)	($31,502)
Total Interest Payment	**($28,877)**	**($13,747)**	**($4,431)**	**($2,630)**
Interest as a % of amount financed	46%	29%	12%	8%
Primary Costs	**($741)**	**($561)**	**($450)**	**($375)**
Savings	$0	$15,131	$24,446	$30,748

Your credit score is basically a risk assessment. It is used by lenders to get a sense of your risk of repayment, which helps the lender determine the interest they are going to charge you. If your score is below 640, you're what they consider a sub-prime borrower. If your score is above that, you're a prime borrower. There's also another category called deep sub-prime who are folks with scores closer to 500. Borrowers with scores higher than 780 fall into the super prime category.

Let's look at financing a new car using the table above. The cost of an average new car in America is about $37,000. In the table, the offer price is $35,000 and let's assume that you were able to get a slightly lower purchase price. When you are buying a car, the dealership will also include the cost of registration, taxes, and tags in your acquisition cost (that's if you don't pay for them separately), which increases the amount that you will need to borrow. Now let's say you make a small down payment of $3,000 which means that you are looking to borrow $33,000.

If your credit score is in the deep sub-prime category, the average rate a lender will charge you is a 16% APR. The average length of a car note is now over 60 months vs. the 48-month term that it was many years ago. Some loans even go out to 72 or 84 months. Since car dealers know that most buyers will have a monthly payment they can afford in mind, you have to be careful when you are financing a car, because the dealer can just extend the term of the loan to make the monthly payments fit your number. While this may make you feel good, it will dramatically increase the total amount of interest that you will pay over the life of the loan. That is why when you walk into a dealership the sales person usually asks, "What's your number?" What he or she is asking is what monthly payment works for you? Is it $500? $600? $700?

If you're in the deep subprime category, you could easily get a 20% APR, which would make your payment $740 per month. This means you're borrowing $33,000 and paying the lender $62,000 in total payments, *which is almost twice the cost of the car.* While this might seem crazy, it *happens all the time,* because 40% of all auto financing is done at the subprime level. In the regular sub-prime category, the APR is about 10%, which re-

---

If your credit score is in the deep sub-prime category, the average rate a lender will charge you is a 16% APR. The average length of a car note is now over 60 months vs. the 48-month term that it was many years ago.

---

quires you to pay $13,000 of interest payments over the life of the loan. From a monthly payment standpoint, it's almost $200 less than what a deep sub-prime buyer would have to pay, which might not seem like a big deal but it would ultimately save you $15,000 of interest.

That's money that you could put toward funding ownership and legacy. The folks with prime and super prime
credit scores often put more money down and get the
best APRs, (3.6% and 2.5% respectively) with dramatically lower monthly payments and total interest.

	Deep Sub Prime	Sub Prime	Prime	Super Prime
Insurance	250	250	250	250
Parking	200	200	200	200
Tolls	60	60	60	60
Miles per day	40	40	40	40
Miles per Month	1200	1200	1200	1200
Fuel efficiency Miles/Gallon	18	30	30	40
Tank size	14	14	14	14
Miles per Tank	252	420	420	560
Tanks per Month	4.8	2.9	2.9	2.1
Fuel Cost/Gallon	3.15	3.15	3.15	3.15
Cost per Tank	44	44	44	44
Fuel Cost per Month	210	126	126	94.5
Maintenance	150	150	150	150
Secondary Costs	**($870)**	**($786)**	**($786)**	**($755)**
Primary Cost	($741)	($561)	($450)	($375)
Total Cost of Ownership	**($1,611)**	**($1,347)**	**($1,236)**	**($1,130)**
		$264	$375	$482

When we think about the cost of a car, we usually
think about principal and interest, i.e., the car note or
monthly payment. As you can see from the table immediately preceding this paragraph there are also a
number of other significant costs to owning a car. You
are required to have auto insurance, you may have

to pay tolls during your daily commute and you may also have parking costs or tickets. If you live in a major US city, the cost of parking can be very expensive. Cars also require regular maintenance, which can also be quite expensive. It can also be costly to fill up the tank depending on the car's fuel economy and the daily distance you drive. These expenses must be taken into account. You should not look only at the initial cost, and think, "okay, I can handle that," when the secondary costs can be significantly more than the cost of your car payments.

Some lucky folks may not have to deal with many of these costs because they are subsidized by their parents. Perhaps they live at home and don't have to worry about parking. Perhaps their parents cover their insurance, maintenance, or their down payment. While not everyone is in a position to have their family subsidize their costs, those who are should take full advantage of it and allocate every dollar they don't have to spend to funding ownership and legacy. In any case, being an informed buyer can lead to significant savings and help you avoid being locked into costly long term mistakes that dramatically reduce your ability to leave the kind of legacy that you want.

TAKE A VACATION AND SAVE MONEY

Are there other ways to save money and reduce costs? Absolutely, let's talk about vacations because at some point, we all need one.

> " A few years ago, we took a family vacation to Disney World and were able to save quite a bit of money. Here's how we did it. While the price of admission to the various Disney parks is quite expensive, we were able to lower the cost by getting a corporate discount from a family friend and using hotel points that I had accumulated to book a suite at a hotel that was close to the park. The points helped us offset the cost of a suite that was spacious and had its own kitchen. Since the suite had a kitchen, we decided to cook our meals instead of getting room service and eating out. Why? Because we were aware that, while on vacation, a family of four can easily pay about $185 a day on food, which adds up to approximately $1,300 after seven days.
>
> As luck would have it, there was a big box store within a few miles of the hotel and we were able to buy enough groceries for a week for about $250. Compare that to spending $20 per person per day for breakfast and it adds up to a significant savings. Ultimately our vacation goal was for the kids to enjoy Mickey and Minnie, the fireworks, the park, the rides and have a great time and not for Mommy and Daddy to spend over $1,000 on food."

When you're on vacation the hotel room and food aren't the only costs; you'll probably also need a rental car. Being the good steward that you are, you do your research and find a great deal. You're excited because the car is $19 a day and you pat yourself on the back. But when you get to the counter the clerk asks if you want insurance that covers the cost of re-pair or replacement of the rental in case you have an accident. At $19 a day, adding this coverage might be a good idea and your rental would still be affordable. You decide to get the insurance. As the clerk explains the insurance, he lists four different kinds of additional coverage that seem really important to add:

- ✓ **Loss-Damage Waiver (aka collision damage waiver)**
- ✓ **Liability Coverage**
- ✓ **Personal Accident Insurance**
- ✓ **Personal Effects Coverage**

By the time you walk out you have a rental contract that will ultimately *cost hundreds of dollars more than you expected.* Why? Because insurance is protection and it always seems like a prudent and wise thing to have, es-pecially if you are away from home. However, you could be paying for this coverage twice. If you own a car and have full coverage, it's likely that you already have this insurance. You already have collision and liability since these are basic coverages required by many states for its drivers. So what should you do? Call your insurance agent or review your current insurance policy to see if you are already covered. Ask your agent what you should do when you go on your trip and they will explain your coverage to you. Imagine that, a simple phone call can save $300 per trip.

Suppose you have to take a few unexpected trips over the course of a year. You may need to visit a sick family member, attend a funeral, or travel for an unforeseen reason. Four trips could cost you $1,200 in unnecessary rental car expenses.

> By the time you walk out you have a rental contract that will ultimately cost hundreds of dollars more than you expected

There are also ways to drive down the costs of airline tickets, hotel rooms, and rental cars by using points earned from your credit card. The way it works is that you can accumulate points based on how much you spend on a credit card. The catch is that these cards tend to have much higher interest rates than cards with no points. The higher rates are how they recoup the money they spend giving you the points. However, if you are in a position to pay off your credit card debt in full at the end of the month, you won't need to worry about the higher interest rates because you won't be carrying a balance. This puts you in a position to earn points for things you've already budgeted for without paying additional interest. This could end up being a great deal for you.

> ❝ When we got married, my wife used points from her AMEX card that she had accumulated over a number of years to buy the airline tickets for our honeymoon. Several years ago, I had job that required a lot of global travel and I was able to accumulate a significant amount of airline and hotel points. Over the years, I've used those points to offset the costs of family vacations and the vacations that my wife and I took without the kids. We've taken first class vacations to Paris and Rome that would have cost over $25,000 per trip but cost us nothing because we used our credit card points and hotel points. This allowed us to vacation in style at discount prices."

ADDITIONAL WAYS TO SAVE MONEY

There are many other ways that you can save money. Almost everyone who has a car or a home also has, or is required to have, insurance coverage. If you are one of the many people who have both a car and a home, there could be a significant opportunity for you to save some additional money. The first way is to bundle your insurance, which means having the same company provide insurance coverage for your car and home (and other assets). Insurance companies will normally provide a discount on your premiums if you give them more business. The second way is by comparing your current coverage, and the premium that you are paying for that coverage, to what other insurers are offering for the same coverage. Please note that the comparison must be for the same coverage for a true "apples to apples" view. This will ensure that you are paying the lowest premium for the coverage that you have and could save you another $1,200 a year, or $100 per month.

Many people spend over $200 per month, or $2,400 per year, on their cable bills, which is a significant amount of money. For a $50,000 per year household, that is the equivalent of 6.4% of their income on a pre-tax basis. If you eliminate premium and basic cable channels, you could save $100 per month. Since there are many new online services that deliver your favorite programing to you whenever you want at a fraction of the cost, it's worth exploring.

Another opportunity to save money would be to stop playing the lottery. Why? Because Americans spend about $70 billion per year on lottery tickets, which is more than they spend on movie tickets, sport tickets, books, video games and music *combined*. This means that the average adult American spends about $300 per year on lottery tickets and in certain states, like Rhode Island, the number is closer to $800 per year.

Considering that your chances of winning are infinitesimally small (e.g., one in 292 million for the Powerball), it is an extremely unwise use of hard earned money. In the case of the average lottery ticket buyer in Rhode Island, if they invested the $800 per year over 35 years they would have $75,000 at the end of that period. This is a significant amount that could be added to their legacy

.

10 WAYS TO SAVE UP TO $20,000

So, we've talked about a number of ways to reduce cost and increase your cash flow. Let's review them below:

✓ Better car-buying decisions	$5,570 per car
✓ Capture every pay increase	$816 to $3,900 per year
✓ Pack a lunch	$3,600 per year
✓ Shop at discounts stores	$2,000 per year
✓ Reduced insurance cost (autos, home, and car rentals)	$1,500 per year
✓ Eliminate your cable bill	$1,200 per year
✓ Claim Earned Income Tax Credit if eligible	$1,100 per year
✓ Claim property tax exemption for seniors	$1,000 per year
✓ Have kids take lunch to school	$1,000 per child per year
✓ Stop purchasing lottery tickets	$300 per year

These savings can easily add up to $20,000 depending on your circumstances. While saving money is necessary, it is not sufficient in and of itself to build wealth. If you want to build wealth there are two things that you can do with the money you save:

(1) Allocate it to Ownership (eliminating debt)
(2) Allocate it to Legacy (retirement, leaving an inheritance, and addressing a need)

With a legacy mindset, the goal is always the same—increase cash flow, fund ownership, and legacy. No matter how big or small the cash flow increase, always allocate it to funding ownership and legacy. Remember, what we do with $50, we do with $5,000, we do with $50,000, we do with $500,000.

CHAPTER 5

How To Allocate Cash Flow To Fund Ownership And Legacy

S o, you've maximized all available tax benefits, found opportunities to reasonably and sustainably reduce your expenses, and you've increased your cash flow. Good job! The question now is, what do you do with it? How do you put it to its highest and best use?

First, let's put things in perspective. Suppose your initial cash flow from your fully burdened budget was $450 per month. With your new stewardship mindset firmly in place, you examined each line item and found additional savings of $300 per month by locating and reducing your phantom expenses, packing a lunch for yourself and your kids, and lowering your monthly cable bill. That's $3,600 per year of incremental cash flow. Think about it this way, to get $3,600 of cash flow you would need to earn an extra $5,000 per year of income and then pay 25% of it in taxes, so you could have $3,600 left over to use. This is huge, because, if you're a $50,000 per year household, you just gave yourself the equivalent of a 10% raise. If you're a $90,000 a year household, you just gave yourself the equivalent of a 6% raise. That's a 6% to 10% raise versus the 2% raise you might normally get at work. Bravo, well done! Now the challenge is how to allocate your cash flow to fund ownership and legacy.

Funding ownership is primarily about allocating cash flow to accelerate the elimination of your outstanding household debt. Funding legacy is primarily about allocating cash flow to (1) maximize your ability to retire with dignity, (2) leave a sizable inheritance for your children's children, and (3) be a blessing to those in need.

TO GIVE ABUNDANTLY, FOCUS ON STEWARDSHIP, OWNERSHIP, AND LEGACY

When the Israelites were in bondage in Egypt they had nothing of their own. Their labor was not their own, they're homes were not their own, they had no assets of their own, and they possessed no land. They owned nothing and their legacy was bondage. When they left Egypt, they did so with great wealth and eventually took possession of a new land, which they owned outright. In this new land, they had no king to pay tribute to, no government to tax them, no tribute to pay to foreign nations, and no debt on their land. *They owned 100% of their land, 100% of their means of production, and 100% of what they produced.* They were required to give 10% of what they produced to people who had no land and no means of production, i.e., the priests, the widows, the fatherless, and the foreigners. The priests received tithes every year in exchange for their service, while the widows, the fatherless, and the foreigners received tithes every three years. The Israelites used their resources to facilitate trade and became a mighty nation with a strong financial core.

These days, most people have large claims on their income, with taxes and debt payments easily consuming 50% of their earnings, while living expenses and high consumption take the remainder. Today, *what allows people who have limited resources to give freely and abundantly is a mindset focused on stewardship, ownership, and legacy and an environment that complements that mindset.* We are often taught that stewardship means giving, but stewardship is actually about managing your limited resources to their highest and best use in order to deliver an increase on those resources. *In too many cases the emphasis is placed on the act of giving instead of the actions that allow people to be able to give.* This creates a disconnect between your desire to give and your ability to do so. If you want to be able to give in a powerful way, you should focus on stewardship, ownership, and legacy.

Studies show that the average American tithes 2.5% of their annual earnings. This is not surprising since nearly half of all Americans have $0 saved for retirement[xxxiv] and 62% of Americans have no emergency savings for things like a $1,000 emergency room visit or a $500 car repair. Studies also show that about 5% of the U.S. adult population tithes 10% or more of their annual earnings. While tithing at the 10% level is very difficult to do, the data below[xxxv] indicate that people in this group share certain important characteristics — they all have a strong financial core, and a mindset focused on stewardship, ownership, and legacy:

STEWARDSHIP

People who give 10% or more of their income demonstrate financial discipline across all income levels

- **27 % have household incomes under $50K**
- **26 % have incomes from $50K-$75K**
- **21 % have incomes from $75K-$100K**
- **26 % have incomes over $100K**

OWNERSHIP

People who give 10% or more of their income have very little debt

- **80 % have no unpaid credit card bills**
- **74 % have no car payments**
- **48 % have no mortgage payment**
- **28 % are completely debt-free**

LEGACY

People who give 10% or more of their income have significant resources to leave an inheritance for their children's children

- **23 % have net assets of $250K-$500K**
- **20 % have net assets of $500K-$1 million**
- **15 % have net assets over $1 million**
- **80 % have a Will/Estate Plan in place**

While only a small portion of the US population, *people who give 10% or more of their income provide 50% to 80% of all tithes at their respective churches*. Considering this, it would be wise to focus on creating good stewards. A good steward, by definition, is able to give generously because she manages her resources wisely and is focused on increasing ownership and building a legacy. She doesn't need to "borrow from Peter to give to Paul" because her desire to give is fully aligned with her ability to do so.

At the end of the day, if you want to give more generously than you are currently able to, focus on stewardship, ownership, and legacy, and over time, as your cash flow increases, you can increase how much you give.

BE A BLESSING TO THOSE IN NEED

In an earlier example, you started with cash flow of $450 per month and added an additional $300 per month by utilizing a few of the savings strategies we discussed. Now, your total cash flow is $750 per month. A portion of this increased cash flow will go to fund ownership and the remainder will go to funding legacy. As part of funding your legacy you should set aside 10% of your cash flow, which in this case would be $75 per month, or $900 per year, so that when you see a need in your community, you can seed into it and help someone in a profound way.

❝ In applying these principles in our household, my wife and I decided to proactively set aside 10% of our current cash flow and 10% of our incremental cash flow so we could be a blessing to someone in need. Several winters ago, while we were driving to church, we saw a young man and his son walking through the snow. They were well dressed and, given the time and the day, it seemed like they were heading to church. They looked familiar, but we weren't sure if we had seen them at our church or in another social setting. It was quite cold outside and there was a lot of snow on the ground. While we weren't sure who they were, we turned the car around and went back to pick them up on the off chance that they might be heading to our church. It turned out that they did go to our church and were on their way to the 11:00 AM service.

When we arrived at church, they thanked us for the ride. We offered to give them a ride home after the service but they said that they already had a ride. Later that evening, my wife and I talked about what had transpired that day. Seeing this young brother walking miles to get to church in the freezing cold with his son, while so many of his peers are literally walking away from the church and not present in their children's lives, was profound. It struck such a chord within us that we decided to try to find a way to help them. We decided to talk to our pastor to get an understanding of the young man's situation. We then invited him to dinner to learn more about him and his son. As we talked, I told him about my life, my upbringing, and about growing up without a father. He in turn told me about his life, which was filled with struggles, challenges, and heartbreak. He grew up not knowing what it was like to feel loved, was around drugs and violence, and his father was also not present. He was determined to do everything in his power to ensure that his son would have a better life. His son's mother was struggling with drug addiction, so he fought for custody of his son. He had dropped out of college several years prior but had recently returned to complete his degree, while working full time. However, without a car, he was struggling to get back and forth to school, work, and to after school care for his son. Yet, with all this, he still had a strong faith and a deep desire to help the least among us.

Later that evening, after he left, my wife and I discussed our conversation and we decided to invest in him and his future. From what I had learned, it seemed that his ability to keep his job, complete his degree, and keep custody of his son all hinged on having transportation, so we decided to get him a modest used car. I talked with our pastor and enlisted the help of the owner of an auto dealership who attends our church and helped us secure a reliable used car at an excellent price.

We funded the purchase of the car and gave it to him. He was shocked and overwhelmed and incredibly grateful for what we had done. I became his mentor and over the next few years there would be many challenges and triumphs. We were blessed to watch him graduate from college with a 3.6 GPA, enter a master's program, get married, and expand his family.

Because we had proactively and intentionally set aside resources, we were able to make a small investment in the life of an extraordinary young man who was trying hard, in the face of significant adversity, to do the right thing. That small investment will help establish a foundation that will add millions to his lifetime earnings and change the trajectory of his children and their children. The idea is that seeding is not just blind giving, it's about doing what you can to seed into transformation and intergenerational change".

WHAT IS DEBT?

After you set aside $75 per month for seeding, allocate the remaining $675 per month to ownership and legacy. Maximizing ownership requires that you eliminate your household debt. Eliminating your household debt requires a plan. For the plan to be effective, you must understand what debt is and the landscape of debt that surrounds us.

Debt, quite simply, is an obligation that must be repaid. I bet you thought I was going to hit you with a long, super-technical definition of what debt is. Nope. It's just an obligation that must be repaid. In this chapter, we'll discuss financial debts, but there are other kinds of debts, for instance, a debt of gratitude. Have you ever heard someone say, "I'm forever in your debt?" They mean a sense of gratitude, so profound, that even though *you* don't require repayment, *they* require it of themselves.

Most of us, except for a privileged few, are quite familiar with financial debt. However, if you truly want to understand debt, you're going to have to think about something even more basic, which is trade. Trade is the exchange of goods and services between different parties. If you have something that I want, and I have something that you want, we can decide to exchange them. If there's no money involved, it's called bartering, which is old school… like, *really* old school. Nowadays, there's always money involved and that begs the question, what is money? *Money is basically something that represents the value of a good or service.*

Suppose we're in a situation where you don't have something to trade that I want, but I have something that you want. Well, that trade is not going to happen. However, if there is something that you have that is equivalent to what I want, (which is what money represents), then we can make the trade happen. That's fundamentally what money is; *something that represents the value of a good or service and makes trading more efficient.* Now, suppose in another situation, you have what I want but I don't have enough goods and services to make the trade. What's going to happen? The short answer is nothing. That trade ain't gonna happen and I'll just have to come back when I have enough money to make the trade.

Let's say, that the thing you have that I need is food. Then that trade is definitely going to happen since I need food to live. Or let's say, I'm going to war and the things you have that I need are weapons and armaments. Again, that trade is definitely going to happen. How is it going to happen? Even though I don't have enough goods and services, I'm going to find a way to entice you to do the trade because I need the food and weapons. I'm going to make you a promise that I will pay you the difference, with my future earnings. Now, you're going to think about me and carefully consider the whole history of our relationship and whether you feel confident that I will repay you. But for you to do the trade, you're probably going to require a couple of things from me. The first thing you are going to require is a fee, because you're not getting what you want up front. You'll get it sometime in the future, which is an inconvenience, and you're going to need compensation for that inconvenience. That fee is called interest or usury.

Debt, quite simply, is an obligation that must be repaid.

The second thing you'll need is a security. Even if we go *way* back and you love me to death… stuff happens. And if stuff happens, you still need to get what's owed to you. So I will need to make you feel "secure" by putting up something of equivalent value as a guarantee. This security effectively becomes your property if I cannot make good on my promise. In the past, it would be something physical, like a house, oxen, a cart, weapons, or it might have been a person, a family member or even yourself.

Let's think deeply about debt. *When you establish a debt, you are fundamentally transferring ownership of your future earnings to someone else.* That's essentially what you're doing. When you transfer a portion of your future earnings, you now *"owe"* your lender. If you transfer all or more of your future earnings, then they now *"own"* you. If they get to determine what your future earnings will be, then they own you forever.

Let that wash over you for a minute. *You are transferring a portion of your future earnings to someone else.* Our focus, and our charge, is to leave an inheritance for our children's children. This is a huge and audacious goal that is bigger than ourselves. It means that, not only are you and your children provided for, but that you're also working to provide an inheritance for *their* children. *When you take on debt, a portion of that inheritance is transferred away from them and shifted to someone else.*

While *stewardship leads to ownership, debt reduces ownership and transfers legacy.* So we have to be very careful, as stewards, with how we're engaging with and accumulating debt. This is a very deep concept. Consider what the Bible[xxxvi] says about debt and borrowing and lenders and things of that nature. The words "own/owner" shows up about 665 times in the NIV version of the Bible. That's a lot of repetition, so it must be important. If you also look at the word "posses," which is just another word for ownership, it shows up 63 times.

What about the word borrow? How many times does that show up? The words borrow and borrower show up about eight times. Since repetition is key to learning and ownership shows up a lot but borrowing does not, perhaps we should put our focus on owning instead of borrowing. If you look at a few instances when the Bible talks about borrowing and lending, you'll notice a very clear theme. In Deuteronomy, borrowers are viewed in an unenviable light and lenders are viewed in a positive light. "You will lend to many nations but will borrow from none. The Lord will make you the head and not the tail.[xxxvii]" So, if you follow the principles outlined here, what happens? You will lend to many nations but will borrow from none.

"And the Lord will make you the head and not the tail. With obedience, you'll be the lender, not the borrower, and the head, and not the tail." Let's look at what happens with disobedience:

> *"The foreigners who reside among you*
> *will rise above you higher and higher, but*
> *you will sink lower and lower. They will lend to*
> *you, but you will not lend to them. They will*
> *be the head and you will be the tail"*
> —*Deuteronomy 28:43-44 (NIV)*

That's very powerful. *The lender is in a position of power and of authority.* If you think about it, that makes a lot of sense. *To lend, you must have abundance.* You don't lend what you need to survive. *You lend the surplus that you've accumulated. So, a lender is in an enviable position.* It's a position of leadership, which is why they say you will be the head, because the head leads the body. With obedience, you are the lender and not the borrower. And with disobedience, it's the other way around. It's very clear that being a borrower is not a position that you should be in. Proverbs states that, "the rich will rule over the poor and the borrower is slave to the lender.[xxxix]" Think about that. *The borrower is slave to the lender.* With disobedience, you end up being the borrower. In Deuteronomy, it's actually a curse because, as the borrower, you're continually transferring ownership to someone else who will rule over you.

UNDERSTANDING THE DEBT LANDSCAPE

Let's consider where we are as borrowers. US households have over $12 trillion of debt. This debt includes first mortgages, Home Equity Lines of Credit (HELOC), credit cards, auto loans, student loans, plus other debts. By the way, a trillion is a thousand billion. Clearly, $12 trillion is a lot of debt.

If you looked at US household debt in 2003, it was $7 trillion. Today, it's over $12 trillion which is a tremendous increase in just 13 years. The biggest portion of our current debt is from our homes, which is about $9 trillion. Homes are expensive, and very few of us have the upfront cash to buy them outright, so we borrow money to do so. We have an additional $1 trillion in auto loans, with 40% of all those loans being issued at sub-prime rates, which means that many people are paying very high rates to have a car and, at times, paying back *double the actual cost of the car* in fees. We also have $1 trillion of student loans with college students taking out $100 billion in student loans each year and almost $1 trillion of credit card debt.

African American Income Distribution

❏ **Less than $12,500**   **22%**
❏ **$12,500 to $37,499**   **37%**
❏ **$37,500 to $62,499**   **19%**
❏ **$62,500 to $87,499**   **12%**
❏ **$85,000 to $112,499**   **5%**
❏ **Greater than $112,500**   **5%**

The data above is from the U.S. Bureau of Labor Statistics and shows the income distribution for African-American households in 2010–2012. It starts at $12,500 or less, and goes all the way up to greater than $112,500. You can see that our incomes are skewed to the lower income levels with 22% of African-American households earning less than $12,000 annually. That's an extraordinarily low earnings level for a household. Another 37% earn between $12,500 and $37,500. This means that almost 60% of African-American households earn less than $37,500 annually, with another 36% making between $37,500 and $112,500.

Another 5% of African-American households earn more than $112,500 annually and represent the wealthiest households in the African-American community. You might expect these folks to carry less debt in general, and less credit card debt in particular, but that is not the case. Surprisingly, 80% of them have household debt and almost 50% of them carry credit card balances month to month and use 21% of their income to pay debt.

FUNDING OWNERSHIP BY ELIMINATING YOUR DEBT

African-Americans earn $1.2 trillion per year and spend an average of 23% of that income on debt service. This means that we are spending approximately $276 billion per year on debt. That is enough money to double all tithing, fund every African-American student in college, completely rebuild all 100 historical Black colleges with world-class, cutting-edge facilities, provide financing for millions of Black business, and still have money left over. This is why we must establish a plan to eliminate all of that debt and free up a massive amount of cash flow to fund ownership and legacy and benefit our community.

Sun Tzu, the great Chinese philosopher and military strategist, said, "Strategy without tactics is the longest path to victory. Tactics without strategy is the noise before defeat." What he meant is if you have a goal or destination without a well laid out plan, but you're persistent, you might eventually get there. You might have gray hair when you do, but eventually you might get there. Tactics without a strategy is another matter altogether—all that you're doing is making a lot of noise and your defeat is certain.

To successfully eliminate debt, we must have an effective plan and well-defined goals. The first step is to list all of your current debts, including principal outstanding, monthly payments, and interest rates. The next step is to create a plan to eliminate all of that debt. Why? Because debt consumes too much of our income and transfers too much of our legacy to our lenders. *If you eliminate your debt, not only will you have full ownership of your property but you could also give yourself the equivalent of a 30%[xl] raise in the process.* This will allow you to dramatically increase your ability to leave a sizable legacy for your children's children.

Creditor	Balance	Rate	Payment	Interest
Card #1	6,762	25.0%	200	141
Card #2	5,500	23.0%	150	105
Card #3	3,500	21.0%	85	61
Auto Loan #1	14,641	6.5%	350	79
Auto Loan #2	12,500	7.5%	295	78
Student Loan #1	31,172	4.3%	225	111
Student Loan #2	17,000	4.3%	110	61
1st Mortgage	133,614	5.0%	850	551
2nd Mortgage	35,000	6.8%	400	197
Total	$259,689		$2,665	$1,385

Creditor	Original Balance	Total Interest Paid	Years to Pay Off
Card #1	6,762	5,059	5.0
Card #2	5,500	4,086	5.3
Card #3	3,500	2,747	6.2
Auto Loan #1	14,641	2,007	4.0
Auto Loan #2	12,500	2,067	4.2
Student Loan #1	31,172	11,939	16.0
Student Loan #2	17,000	7,785	18.8
1st Mortgage	133,614	82,229	21.2
2nd Mortgage	35,000	13,324	10.1
Total:	$259,689	$131,243	

In the scenario above you see debt for a family of four. Let's say the husband makes $37,000 per year and the wife makes $53,000 for a combined household income of $90,000. They have three credit cards with a cumulative balance of $15,000. Coincidentally, $15,000 is the average balance for all U.S. credit card holders. They have two auto loans that total $27,000 and two student loans totaling $48,000. They also have a first and second mortgage, which total $170,000.

In total, their debts add up to $260,000 with monthly payments of $2,665. This family is spending about 35% of their total income on debt. The number they should be most concerned about is the almost $1,400 per month that they are paying in interest. So, while they are paying $2,700 per month on debt, only about $1,300 is going to reducing their principal. At the current rate and pace, if they keep paying this way, it will take about 21 years to pay off this debt. This assumes that they don't add any new debt as they make these payments, otherwise it could take much, much longer. Not adding any new debt sounds easy in theory, but can be quite difficult in practice. It's important to note that the $15,000 of credit card debt that the average credit card holder owes, has not changed much in the last 10 years. This means that most credit card holders are continually adding new debt as they pay down existing debt. In this example, they're not going to add any new debt because they're committed to ownership and legacy.

How much interest are they going to pay over the next 21 years? Unfortunately, it's going to be about $131,000, which is a huge sum of money. The main problem is that the $131,000 comes from their future earnings and is money that will be shifted from their legacy to their lenders.

It's crucial that they find a way to minimize the amount of resources that are being shifted away from legacy. The interest they are paying is a function of two things, the amount of debt that's outstanding and the time it takes to pay it back. In this scenario, since they can't reduce the amount they owe, they will need to minimize the time it takes to pay it back. Sounds simple but how can they do it? The first step is a full commitment to not add any new debt. Period. The second step is to apply a methodology called a debt waterfall. A debt waterfall is a simple but powerful tool. With it, as you pay off one debt, instead of allocating that payment to additional spending, add it to the amount that you are already paying on another debt. After the next debt is paid off, take the last two payments and apply them to another debt and so on.

Debt waterfall is a transformative and very powerful tool because combining payments greatly accelerates your ability to pay off each subsequent debt. If they did those things (i.e., not adding new debt and utilizing the debt waterfall) and nothing else, what would be the impact? The impact would be substantial and far reaching. As you'll see in the chart below, if they used the debt waterfall, they would save $41,000 in total interest and would be able to shift that $41,000 to leaving a legacy. They would also have the added benefit of paying off their debt in half the time—11 years.

Creditor	Original Balance	Total Interest Paid	Years to Pay Off
Card #1	6,762	4,880	4.3
Card #2	5,500	3,888	4.4
Card #3	3,500	2,475	4.5
Auto Loan #1	12,500	2,067	4.2
Auto Loan #2	35,000	9,876	5.8
Student Loan #1	14,641	2,007	4.0
Student Loan #2	133,614	47,636	10.3
1st Mortgage	31,172	10,285	10.7
2nd Mortgage	17,000	6,163	10.9
Total	$259,689	$89,277	

Now you might be thinking, "Wow, that sounds awesome, but which debt should they pay off first?

Should they pay the largest debt? The smallest debt? The highest interest rate debt?" Good questions. I would encourage them to start with the highest interest rate debt first, because it's burning a hole in their pocket. They have a credit card with a 25% interest rate, but it's really much higher than 25%, because they are paying the 25% with after-tax money. Think about it this way, they have to earn 32%, and pay taxes on it, so they can have the 25% left to pay the interest on the debt. This means their rate is more like 32% on a before tax basis, which is crazy. *This is a huge negative return and there are often no better investments than getting rid of high interest rate debt.* However, some people need to see progress early on because, psychologically, it gives them a sense of accomplishment, which helps them to stay the course and not give up. In this case, it may be better for them to start with the lowest balance, so they can pay it off and move on to the next debt.

Let's kick it up a notch. What would happen if they took $300 of their $750 monthly cash flow and added it to the $2,665 per month that they are currently paying? Their total monthly payment would be $2,995 per month and is being applied in a debt waterfall fashion. That would save them another $20,000 of interest payments. Instead of paying $131,000 in interest, they will now only pay $70,000. That's a $60,000 cost reduction. Huge, right?

Creditor	Original Balance	Total Interest Paid	Years to Pay Off
Card #1	6,762	1,263	1.4
Card #2	5,500	1,982	2.0
Card #3	3,500	1,455	2.3
Auto Loan #1	12,500	1,769	2.8
Auto Loan #2	35,000	7,619	4.4
Student Loan #1	14,641	2,007	4.0
Student Loan #2	133,614	39,602	8.5
1st Mortgage	31,172	9,199	9.0
2nd Mortgage	17,000	5,482	9.3
Total	$259,689	$70,377	

They now have a viable plan to be debt-free in nine years. If they allocate $300 per month, over the course of nine years they can generate $60,000 in interest savings and almost $3,000 per month of incremental cash flow. In nine years, they will own 100% of their assets and will have given themselves the equivalent of a 46% raise.

FUNDING LEGACY

After setting aside $75 per month to seed into those in need, and $300 per month to accelerate their debt repayment, they still have $375 per month of cash flow. But we should also look at where they are in terms of retirement savings. Their goal is to maximize the amount of income-generating assets they'll have when they stop working. They will need enough to be able to provide for themselves and also help their grandchildren. To be able to do this, they'll need about 20 times their salary in retirement savings generating a 5% annual return.

Let's assume that our couple is 35 years old and that they would like to retire at age 65, which gives them 30 years to maximize their retirement assets. While they don't have much extra cash, let's assume that they have managed to sock away a total of $15,000 in their respective employer sponsored 401k plans and are currently contributing 2% of their salary into their respective 401k plans. Let's also assume that their employers have matching programs, where they will match 50% of every $1 our couple contributes, up to 3% of their salary. Since their combined salaries are $90,000 per year, that means that their companies will contribute up to a combined amount of $2,700 per year to their retirement plans.

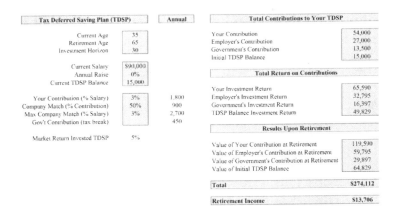

Tax Deferred Saving Plan (TDSP)		Annual		Total Contributions to Your TDSP	
Current Age	35			Your Contribution	54,000
Retirement Age	65			Employer's Contribution	27,000
Investment Horizon	30			Government's Contribution	13,500
				Initial TDSP Balance	15,000
Current Salary	$90,000				
Annual Raise	0%			Total Return on Contributions	
Current TDSP Balance	15,000				
				Your Investment Return	65,590
Your Contribution (% Salary)	3%	1,800		Employer's Investment Return	32,795
Company Match (% Contribution)	50%	900		Government's Investment Return	16,397
Max Company Match (% Salary)	3%	2,700		TDSP Balance Investment Return	49,829
Gov't Contribution (tax break)		450			
				Results Upon Retirement	
Market Return Invested TDSP	5%				
				Value of Your Contribution at Retirement	119,590
				Value of Employer's Contribution at Retirement	59,795
				Value of Government's Contribution at Retirement	29,897
				Value of Initial TDSP Balance	64,829
				Total	$274,112
				Retirement Income	$13,706

You can see in the table above that on their current trajectory, assuming their investments earn an average return of 5% per year over the course of their investment, they'll have $274,112 of assets at retirement generating an income of $13,706 per year. This obviously will not be enough to retire on, but it does provide a good starting point for them to work with.

There is another problem they may not be aware of. While their employers are willing to contribute $2,700 per year, our couple is only getting $900 of that amount. They are losing $1,800 of matching contributions each year along with the 5% interest that they could have been earning. To improve this situation, there are two important things that our couple can do. The first is to add the $375 per month of cash flow from their fully burdened budget to the current amount of cash they are contributing to their 401k's. This will not only increase their total contributions to their 401k's but will also help them capture 100% of the money their companies are willing to contribute. The second thing, is to reinvest the tax benefit they receive from putting money into their 401k. For example, if they put $1,000 into their 401k, it will lower their taxable income and could save them $250 in taxes per year. Any money they save in taxes should also be invested for retirement. As you'll see in the table below: if they invest the money that they save in taxes over the next 30 years it could generate another $40,000 of income generating assets at retirement.

Tax Deferred Saving Plan (TDSP)		Annual
Current Age	35	
Retirement Age	65	
Investment Horizon	30	
Current Salary	$90,000	
Annual Raise	0%	
Current TDSP Balance	15,000	
Your Contribution (% Salary)	7%	6,300
Company Match (% Contribution)	50%	2,700
Max Company Match (% Salary)	3%	2,700
Gov't Contribution (tax break)		1,575
Market Return Invested TDSP	5%	

Total Contributions to Your TDSP	
Your Contribution	189,000
Employer's Contribution	81,000
Government's Contribution	47,250
Initial TDSP Balance	15,000

Total Return on Contributions	
Your Investment Return	229,565
Employer's Investment Return	98,385
Government's Investment Return	57,391
TDSP Balance Investment Return	49,829

Results Upon Retirement	
Value of Your Contribution at Retirement	418,565
Value of Employer's Contribution at Retirement	179,385
Value of Government's Contribution at Retirement	104,641
Value of Initial TDSP Balance	64,829
Total	$767,420
Retirement Income	$38,371

Adding $375 per month increases their 401k contributions from 2% to 7% of their salaries. This would allow them to capture the full $2,700 per year that their companies are willing to contribute. Now our couple is putting in $6,300 per year, their companies are contributing another $2,700 per year, and they are also reinvesting their tax benefits. These actions could increase their assets at retirement by approximately $500,000 to $767,000 and in nine years this couple will also be debt-free. This means that they are going to have $2,665 per month (or $32,000 per year) of additional cash flow available for further investment in nine years.

Let's suppose that our couple decided to invest the entire $32,000 per year in their 401k's. Since they are already contributing $6,300 per year into their 401k's, they can contribute another $29,700 per year in their company plans and still receive a tax benefit. They can also put the remaining $2,280 per year into an Individual Retirement Account (IRA). The entire $32,000 per year that was freed up after their debt was eliminated can now be invested at 5% for 21 years, along with an additional $8,000 per year of potential tax savings. This would generate another $1,480,000 at retirement ($1,184,000 plus $296,000 of reinvested tax savings). That amount plus the previous $767,000 would lead to $2,247,000 at retirement that's generating $112,371 per year of income. This is, of course, a best-case scenario. However, even if they did half of what we discussed, they would still be debt-free and completely secure in retirement with a significant legacy to leave for their children's children.

Maximizing your cash flow allows you to accelerate your debt elimination, which in turn dramatically increases your cash flow, and turbo-charges your retirement savings. It is a powerful continuum: stewardship leads to ownership, which ultimately leads to legacy, which is good for your SOuL.

CHAPTER 6

Credit—The Good, The Bad, And The Ugly

I n Chapter 5, we used the power of allocating cash flow to eliminate all household debt in half the time. We then took the cash that was freed up by the elimination of that debt and used it to fund retirement. The result was powerful and had the dual benefit of allowing the couple in our example to retire debt-free and with financial security.

That exercise was important because research indicates that Black American households pay 23% of their income on debt and in our example our couple was paying 35% of their income on debt. The amount of money that Black households pay to service their debt is based on three factors. The first factor is the amount of debt outstanding, the second is the interest rate on that debt, and the third is the length of time it takes to pay the debt back. Since the interest rate (which is your cost of debt) depends on a person's credit history (which is summarized in their credit score), we should take some time to fully understand credit, credit reports and credit scores. This is vital because credit affects your cost of debt, which affects your cash flow, which in turn affects ownership and legacy.

WHAT IS CREDIT?

Credit is the maximum amount of debt that you can incur. It is important to understand the relationship between credit and debt. Credit is how much you can borrow, while debt is how much you have borrowed. From an accounting perspective, credit increases a liability or reduces an asset. If you increase a liability, you are reducing ownership and if you reduce an asset you are reducing legacy.

Credit represents your ability to obtain goods and services before paying for them. The person who extends you the credit is always concerned about getting his or her money back. Therefore, they need to "trust" and be confident that you will follow through on your agreement or your "promise to repay." The best way to get a sense of what someone will do in the future is to look at what he or she has done in the past. Therefore, the best way to get a sense of whether or not someone will pay you back, is to look at whether or not they have paid other people back.

This is where credit reports and credit scores come into play. A credit report lists the types of debt you have, the length of time your accounts have been open, and whether or not you've paid your bills on time. It tells lenders how much credit you've used and if you're opening new sources of credit. In general, it gives lenders a broad and accumulative view of your credit history.[xli]

> # The best way to get a sense of what someone will do in the future is to look at what he or she has done in the past.

A credit score, on the other hand, is a three-digit number that is calculated using information from your credit report that provides a potential lender with a concise piece of information that can be used to quickly determine to what extent they can "trust" you to repay any money they lend you. It helps to answer the question of whether or not you can be trusted to repay your debt in the future based on how you've met your past and present obligations. So, credit is built on trust and trust is based on observing past experience and past performance.

African-American Credit Disparities

In 1999, Freddie Mac did an extensive Consumer Credit Survey (CCS) that had some very interesting findings:

- **48% of African-Americans were deemed to have bad credit**[xlii]
- **23% of Blacks believe they have bad credit but actually do not**
- **Whites who earn $25,000 have better credit that Blacks who earn $65,000 to $75,000**
- **Nearly 60% of Blacks reported having been turned down for a loan or credit card in the past two years**

Why is this important? *Because credit affects the cost of debt and the cost of debt affects our cash flow, which affects our ownership and ultimately our legacy.*

A Brief History of Credit Scores and Reports

Let's talk about the history behind credit reports and credit scores, where they came from and why are they so pervasive. The idea of extending credit, and trying to figure out whether or not you can trust someone to repay you, goes back thousands of years. In the United States, the beginnings of "credit reports" date back to the 1830s when businesses that operated within certain regions or local areas were trying to identify the best customers to extend credit to. Business owners kept track of customers who repaid their debt, and those who didn't, and began to share those records among themselves. Eventually credit bureaus emerged to manage this activity.

These bureaus sprang up in numerous places and over many decades. Over time they consolidated to get better insight on larger and larger numbers of consumers. That process continued into the mid-1950s when two gentlemen, William Fair and Earl Isaac, decided to start a company that used information in these credit bureaus to predict which customers were more likely to repay their debts and which were not. They used sophisticated statistical methods and an emerging technology called "computers" to come up with a number that would help businesses figure out who they could "trust" to repay their debts.

They called the company the Fair, Isaac Corporation, which was later shortened to FICO. Businesses found this service to be quite helpful and soon retail stores started using FICO's services to help extend credit to consumers. These retailers were extending credit without taking any security and it turned out to be a very profitable business for them. This profitability led banks to follow suit and, over the next 30 years, unsecured credit cards became prevalent.

In 1970, Congress passed the Fair Credit Reporting Act (FCRA), which according to the Federal Trade Commission (FTC), was "designed to protect the privacy of consumer report information and to guarantee that the information supplied by consumer reporting agencies is as accurate as possible."[xliii] In the early to mid-'90s, Fannie Mae and Freddie Mac, the giant mortgage companies that most banks and financial institutions sell their mortgages to, decided to require FICO scores/report for mortgage applications. That's the short history of how credit scores and reports became so pervasive.

Understanding Your Credit Score

A FICO score is the output of a credit scoring system that was developed by the FICO company. It is the most widely used scoring system in the country and is used by most banks, mortgage companies, car dealerships, and retailers to determine whether or not they will extend credit and at what rate. FICO scores range from 300 to 850. Poor, Average, Good, and Excellent FICO scores generally fall within the following ranges:

- ❐ **Poor credit is considered a FICO score under 630**
- ❐ **Average or Fair credit is between 630 and 690**
- ❐ **Good Credit is between 690 and 720**
- ❐ **Excellent credit is anything above 720**

There are three bureaus that compile information on the type and amount of debt, total credit available, payment history and other factors, such as tax liens, foreclosures, short sales and bankruptcies. Those companies are Experian, TransUnion, and Equifax. FICO calculates a score based on the credit profile that each of these companies create, so you will have a credit score from each bureau. When FICO calculates a credit score they put a lot of weight on a few key items from your credit report. The biggest item is your payment history because they want to see if you're making your payments on time and if not, they look at how many days late you've been. *Payment history is 35% of your score.*

They then look at how much of the total credit extended to you is being used. The ratio of how much credit you have outstanding and how much you are using is called your utilization rate. If your utilization is low, they love it. If your utilization is high, it will count against you in a big way. Utilization amounts to 30% of your score. *Your utilization and payment history make up 65% of your total score, which is a very big deal.*

Next is the length of your credit history, which is 15% of your score. If you have a long history of timely payments it will be great for your score, but if you don't have much history it will definitely count against you. *Recent credit inquires is another 10% of your total score.* Every time you apply for credit, the company providing the credit will "pull" your credit report and it will show up on your credit report as an inquiry for other companies to see. The more inquiries you have the lower your score will be. Finally, they look at the various types of credit that you have. Do you have a personal loan, a car loan, a mortgage, or credit cards? The type of credit you have accounts for the remaining 10% of your credit score. FICO will look at all of these factors and run them through their unique set of calculations and come up with a three-digit score between 300 to 850, which is your credit score.

Credit: A Proxy for Trust

Across all 141 million U.S. households, the average credit score is about 680. If you're above 800, it's awesome. You're going to get the best rates and lowest cost of debt. If you're below 600, it's going to be very difficult for you to get a loan and, if you do, the rates could be astronomical. Earlier I said that your credit score was a proxy for trust. Let's take another look at that.

The default rate for people with a score of about 830 is basically 0%, while the default rate for people with a 660 is about 30%. From the lenders perspective, when they see applicants with higher scores, they feel more confident that they will get their money back. On the other hand, borrowers with a 660 are almost seven times more likely to default than someone with an 830 credit score. So, they may not be entirely confident they will get their money back and if they do lend to a person with a 660, it will likely be at a higher price.

What's the difference between default and delinquency? Delinquency means that you are behind on payments. Once you are delinquent, you have a certain period of time to get back on track or your lender will declare the loan to be in default. At that point, the entire loan balance will immediately become due. That's the fundamental difference. Credit scores are vital information because they influence a lender's thinking about how trustworthy you are based on your credit history. To the lender, it is less likely that a borrower with a 600 FICO is going to repay them because they have almost a 40% default rate. Because of the increased likelihood of not getting their money back, lenders may not provide any financing to people with a 600 credit score and if they do, they may do so at a very high rate. However, because of their credit history, the lender can be confident that a person with an 800 FICO score is highly likely to pay them back because their default rate is about 1%. So, they'll not only lend to them, they'll do so at a low rate. What about a person with a 700 FICO score? Well, because some of those folks don't pay on time (22% are delinquent) and some don't pay the money back at all (5% are in default), they'll lend to that person but at a higher rate than the person with an 800 score because of those concerns.

The System Is Not Without Flaws

This system is not always without flaws. Lenders don't differentiate between people who are being willfully irresponsible and people who run into very difficult situations. Suppose you lose your job and it takes you six or eight months to find a new one. During that time, it's unlikely you'll be able to pay your bills since most people don't have enough emergency funds to last three weeks between jobs. When something like this happens, you may want to pay your bills and your rent but you can't. *It's difficult when you're dealing with a catastrophic situation like job loss and you're treated the same as someone who is careless or just unwilling to pay in a timely manner even though they can.* At the end of the day, the credit score doesn't differentiate between the two.

It is the same for medical debts. This is a huge area of concern. *America has the highest medical costs in the entire world.* If your medical bills are high and your insurance doesn't cover them, the amount that you owe can deplete your savings and destroy your finances. There are many "well to do" people who had their savings wiped out due to unexpected medical expenses. When that happens, it's not about being irresponsible in any way, shape, or form, but from a credit score perspective, it counts against you just the same. It shouldn't, but it does. In fact, over half the collections on credit reports are due to medical debt. By the way, many of these debts are less than $500, but that still counts against you. So, there are definitely flaws to the system that we must take into consideration. Fair and Isaac created very advanced statistical algorithms to come up with these numbers but the formula is only as good as the input. We should also be very careful to avoid financial mistakes because even small ones add up in a big way.

///

Initially, a credit report was about helping a lender assess how much debt could safely be extended to a borrower, and at what price. Now, credit reports are being used for many other things; one is employment.

///

Research has shown that up to 21% of the information on credit reports is incorrect. Thirteen percent of those mistakes will lower your score and 5% of them are enough to get you declined outright. So be vigilant about what's on your report. What are some of the other financial mistakes people tend to make? We recently came out of the worst economic recession since the Great Depression, which affected millions of people. Many families had to sell their homes for less than they owed on their mortgage. This is called a short sale. While you and the bank agree to do this transaction, the short sale might be incorrectly recorded as a foreclosure.

This is problematic and detrimental because a foreclosure does more damage to your credit score than a short sale. So, we have to be aware of what's on our credit report and check it for inaccuracies. Homeowners may sometimes get a loan modification in which the bank lowers their principal or reduces their interest rate and creates a new mortgage agreement. But the bank might still be reporting to the credit bureaus that you are not paying according to the terms and conditions of the old mortgage agreement. That's clearly a mistake because the old mortgage agreement no longer applies. It's their mistake but you're paying the cost. You must be vigilant and not assume that your information is accurate because research has shown that 21% of the time, that's not the case.

Credit Reports Are Being Used for More Than They Were Designed For

Credit reports are being used for more than what they were initially developed for and this is cause for concern. Initially, a credit report was about helping a lender assess how much debt could safely be extended to a borrower, and at what price. Now, credit reports are being used for many other things; one is employment.

Every job I've had in the corporate sector has required a background check where they pulled my credit report. I've had some very high-level financial roles, so I understand the need to check my credit and fiscal history due to the fiduciary responsibility associated with some of those roles. *Today, almost 50% of employers are pulling credit reports* and the vast majority of those roles don't have any associated fiduciary responsibility, but *10% of the people from a recent study said they were denied employment based on their credit report.*

Unfortunately, millions of credit reports are being pulled for employment purposes despite there not being any documented link between people having low scores and being bad employees, or people having low scores and stealing from their employers. While it certainly doesn't make sense to pull people's credit reports for the vast majority of jobs, it is still quite pervasive. It is important to understand the impact our credit report can have, not only on our cost of debt, but also on our ability to secure employment. This leads to a vicious cycle. If we have debt but can't find a job because of our credit report, we won't be able to pay off that debt.

Your credit score is also being used as one of the variables to determine your auto insurance rate. To establish eligibility for payment plans and to help determine insurance rates, most U.S. insurance companies use credit-based insurance scores along with your driving history, claims history, and many other factors. *The difference* *in cost between someone with a high credit score and low credit score could be $700 per year*. That's substantial. If you own seven cars over your lifetime, which is the average in America, every 10 years, it could cost you an additional $7,000 and you may not even be aware of it.

SMALL MISTAKES HAVE A HUGE IMPACT

It may be difficult to understand how credit scores are calculated and how certain actions might impact your score. As you can imagine, FICO has gotten a lot of questions about this so they put together a chart that gives us a good idea of the kind of score a person with a certain credit profile might have. While they are not going to show you the formula, they will give you an idea of the outcomes. The information listed below is from FICO's website[xliv] and contains some sample information about two profiles:

Alex has a FICO score of 680

❐ Has six credit accounts, including several active credit cards, an active auto loan, a mortgage, and a student loan

❐ An eight-year credit history

❐ Moderate utilization on his credit card accounts (his balances are 40-50% of his limits)

❐ Two reported delinquencies: a 90-day delinquency two years ago on a credit card account, and an isolated 30-day delinquency on his auto loan a year ago

❐ Has no accounts in collections and no adverse public records on file

Benecia has a FICO score of 780

❐ Has 10 credit accounts, including several active credit
cards, an active auto loan, a mortgage and a student loan

❐ A 15-year credit history

❐ Low utilization on her credit card accounts (her balances
are 15-25% of her limits)

❐ Has never missed a payment on any credit obligation

❐ Has no adverse public records on file

Benecia's 780 credit score is pretty good. Alex's
680 credit score is about average. So, what are the
fundamental characteristics that are driving the difference between the two scores?

One of the things that you'll notice is utilization.
Suppose they both had $10,000 worth of outstand-
ing credit. If that is the case, Alex would be using
about $5,000 worth of that credit, which would be a
50% utilization rate. That's considered high because
you should keep the utilization under 30%[xlv]. On the
other hand, Benecia has her utilization at 20% which
is well under 30%. Remember that since utilization
is about 30% of your total credit score it also has a
huge impact on your score. Alex has a much lower
score because of his high utilization.

The biggest factor in the credit score calculation
is driven by your payment history. Unlike Alex, Benecia has never missed a payment. If the payment
is due on the 15th, she pays it like clockwork, on

or before the 15th. Meanwhile, Alex had a 90-day delinquency two years ago and a recent 30-day delinquency on an auto loan. This will lead to another negative impact on Alex's credit score. While neither of them have any collections, the only other major difference is that Benecia has a much longer credit history, which has a positive impact on her score. This all adds up to about a hundred-point difference in their credit scores. A hundred-point difference might not sound like much, but it can have a huge impact on the interest rate that you pay.

The data listed below is also from FICO's website[xlvi] and shows the impact on Alex and Benecia's score, if certain negative things occur and are subsequently recorded on their respective credit reports:

Alex's initial credit score is 680

Alex's credit score after a negative event is added to his credit report:

❒ Maxing out a credit card	650-670
❒ A 30-day delinquency	600-620
❒ Settling a credit card debt	615-635
❒ Foreclosure	575-595
❒ Bankruptcy	530-550
❒ Benecia's initial credit score is	780

Benecia's credit score after a negative event is added to her credit report:

❏ **Maxing out a credit card**   **735-755**

❏ **A 30-day delinquency**   **670-690**

❏ **Settling a credit card debt**   **655-657**

❏ **Foreclosure**   **620-640**

❏ **Bankruptcy**   **540-560**

As you can see, if Alex maxes out his cards (i.e., 100% utilization) his score could drop by 20 points, but if Benecia maxes out her cards, her score would drop by 35 points. *A 30-day delinquency would drop Alex's score by 60 points and Benecia's score by another 100 points, which is huge.* A 30-day delinquency, means that you were supposed to pay your bill on the 15th of last month but you haven't and 30 days passed without the bill being paid. Your lender decided to report it to the credit bureau for all to see, and now it is recorded as a 30-day delinquency. What if Alex settles a credit card dispute for an amount that is less than the balance he originally owed? His score would drop by 55 points. If Benecia did the same thing her score would drop by 115 points. What about a foreclosure? Now, that's really bad news for both of them with Alex's score dropping by 115 and Benecia's score dropping by another 150 points.

So, you can see that lenders put a lot of weight on certain things that are reported. It's important that we as borrowers know that. You can disagree with their formula, you can debate it all you want, but for now, it's the formula and you should protect yourself accordingly. Remember, things that you might think are not a big deal, can be a really big deal, so you don't want any unforced or incorrect errors. Try to deal with unforeseen problems to the best of your ability. *If the ability to pay your debt is within your control, you've got to make sure unnecessary negative information is not reported on your credit report because the impact can be huge and the cost can be severe.*

It is also important to understand that negative information does not stay on your credit report forever. There's only one thing that will be there indefinitely and that's a tax lien. We all have a business partner, which is our friendly neighborhood federal, state, local, and city government that takes a portion of everything that we earn. It's imperative that we pay that portion, especially if it's something like property, sales, or income taxes. If you don't pay them the government can put a tax lien on your home to recover those taxes. Tax liens can have a very negative effect on your credit score and they don't go away unless the government removes them or you pay the taxes that you owe. For everything else, there's a time limit on how long it's going to be on your credit report. The vast majority of negative information comes off your credit report in seven years. Late payments are gone in seven years. If you're supposed to pay today and you don't pay today, you're delinquent. Your lender may not report it that moment, but you don't want to be delinquent past 30 days because it will put you at their mercy and jeopardize your credit.

Bankruptcies are gone in seven years, except for Chapter 7, which is gone after 10 years. Foreclosures are also gone after seven years. If you have collections, they will also stay on your credit report for seven years. The vast majority of negative items will be taken off your credit report after seven years. What you should also know is that the inputs to the credit score calculation are time-dependent. That means, a delinquency that was reported today has a much bigger impact than a delinquency that was reported three years ago. Over time, the impact becomes less damaging and, after seven years it, comes off entirely. It's very important to know that because if you can change your behavior or your circumstances, you can change your credit profile and your score.

The Costs Are Enormous If Your Credit Is Not Well-Managed

If you have poor credit, it can be very difficult to access credit. And if you have trouble obtaining credit, that can set you up to have to deal with companies involved in predatory lending (i.e., providing loans with extremely high rates). There's a whole industry that is lending at immoral rates to people who have the greatest difficulties getting credit. Why do I call it immoral? Because the *Annual Percentage Rates (APR) for predatory loans could be as much as 800% a year.* Yes. 800% per year to the people who have the most difficulty getting loans and the least ability to pay such high rates.

You *must* carefully manage your credit profile because you don't want to expose yourself to high interest loans on cars, personal debt, mortgages, credit cards or student loans. And you certainly don't want to pay more for your auto insurance even though your driving record is excellent, or have difficulty renting the apartment you want, or getting the job that you want or need.

With respect to mortgages, if you get one with a low credit score, your interest rate could be *1% or more higher than folks who have higher credit scores.* A 1% increase in interest might not sound like much, but over 30 years, the impact is astronomical. *That*

1% could cost you $90,000 over the life of your loan, which would significantly reduce your ability to leave an inheritance.

You should also be very careful with auto loans because the difference in interest rates can be huge depending on your credit score. There could easily be a 10-point difference between a high score and a low score. For example, a neighborhood credit union posted rates for borrowers interested in purchasing a new car. To borrow a minimum of $10,000 for 75 months, an applicant with a credit score of 559 or below was offered a rate of 15.24%, while an applicant with a credit score of 740 or more was offered a rate of 2.99%. That amounts to a 12.25 percentage point difference, which is significant.

In order to put that into perspective, the borrower with the 740 score would pay about $2,000 in interest charges over the life of the loan, while the borrower with the 559 credit score would pay almost $16,000 in interest. *The borrower with the 559 credit score is paying about $14,000 more in interest than the borrower with a 740 score.* If we're likely to have seven cars over our lifetime, that could amount to $98,000 of extra cost for a low credit score borrower, which would dramatically reduce their future earnings and decrease their ability to leave a legacy.

HOW TO REPAIR YOUR CREDIT

Your credit history is being recorded and constantly updated. Whether you know it or not doesn't matter. The record is being kept regardless. So, it is important to know your score. Many people don't know their credit scores and most haven't recently looked at their credit report. Keep in mind that the score and the report are two different things. The first thing you should do is to pull your report and see what's in it to ensure that there aren't any mistakes. Because some

> Once you've gotten a copy of your credit report, carefully review it, check for mistakes, and then dispute any you find. Report them to the credit bureau immediately.

of those mistakes will drive our scores down and some will get you denied outright. Since many banks and financial institutions have started providing credit scores to their customers, you may be able to get one or more of your FICO scores on your bank's website. To get a copy of your credit report, you can visit one of the three credit bureaus and request a free copy[xlvii] or use an online credit reporting or credit protection service.

Once you've gotten a copy of your credit report, carefully review it, check for mistakes, and then dispute any you find. Report them to the credit bureau immediately. They will have to substantiate the reported data or remove it. Next, if you're in a financial hole, stop digging. When we're in a hole, the first rule is to stop digging because you'll only get deeper in the hole. Make the commitment to yourself to not add new debt and to not have any more late payments or negative information added to your credit report. If you don't add any new negative marks and resolve your current ones, in seven years, all of your negative information will be gone. Remember, as you are executing your plan to eliminate your debt; as your balance goes down, so does your utilization, *which will significantly increase your score.*

Keep in mind that the process of *paying down your debt increases your credit score.* Suppose you can't get a credit card from a quality credit card company. One thing you can do is to have your bank or financial institution issue you a prepaid card based on the money you have in your account. If you put $500 on your prepaid card, your bank will give you a credit card with a $500 credit limit. As you use the card and make your payments on time, they will report that information to the credit bureau just like a regular credit card, which helps you build credit history and get a higher score over time. While it might sound weird, remember that *time is on your side*. The reason I say that is because seven years is coming no matter what you do. The issue is what position will you be in when it gets here. So, to the extent that it's under your control, make sure that the last time you miss a payment, is the last time you ever miss a payment. It will do wonders for your SOuL.

CONCLUSION

It is my hope that *CPR For The SOuL,* and its powerful financial principles, serve as a catalyst to initiate or renew your commitment to stewardship, ownership, and legacy. While it is true that as a community, we have far fewer resources than we should otherwise have, it is still our duty to manage and grow those resources as best we can. This requires us to increase our wisdom, knowledge, and understanding about personal finances and to develop a mindset that is focused on stewardship, ownership, and legacy. One of the hardest lessons to learn on this journey is that it's not about you. It's about being a good steward of the resources that you have to maximize your ownership of those resources and leave a legacy for not only your children, but also for *their* children.

Stewardship is about getting the highest and best use out of the limited resources that you currently possess so you can maximize your household cash flow. Ownership is about the elimination of all claims to your assets, which in turn maximizes the amount of cash flow available to you. Legacy is about (1) positioning yourself to leave an inheritance for your children's children, (2) having enough resources to retire with dignity, and (3) proactively setting aside money so you can help people who are in need. Renewing and reinforcing that mindset helps you to be in a better position to sacrifice short-term gratification for long-term transformation that impacts not only your family, but also your community.

As you continue along this journey, I encourage you to employ those powerful and empowering principles, methods, and framework to enable your financial success. *When it comes to resources, success is a function of your ability, not your righteousness.* Regardless of what you desire, you have a responsibility to deliver a significant return on what you have or, at the end of the day, it will be taken from you and shifted to those with more ability. Unfortunately, many people ask for and desire more resources than they are capable of managing. *CPR For the SOuL* arms you with the information and knowledge to allow you to not only manage your resources, but to also grow them.

Remember that before you can be an effective help to other people, you must be in a strong position yourself. If you are dissatisfied with your current financial situation and want to change it, you must develop a new mindset, one that is focused on stewardship, ownership, and legacy. You are not going to act differently until you think differently and you're not going to think differently until you believe in something bigger and greater than yourself. Then, when God blesses you with incremental resources, you in turn should be a blessing to someone else. Not only will He honor you, but you will also help those in need and inspire them to be a blessing to others.

Nothing happens in a vacuum. As you improve your ability you must also improve your environment to maximize the outcome associated with your ability. Remember, the three most important factors to someone's ultimate success are (1) where they are born, (2) when they are born, and (3) who they know. Each of those factors represents an important aspect of your environment and, despite conventional thinking, people rarely overcome their environment. They are instead products of that environment. There is no shortage of hard-working people in this world but there is a shortage of productive environments that have a positive multiplier effect on hard work. People who are focused on outcomes without environmental context, are always going to come to the wrong conclusion.

It is vital to develop clear and well-defined goals that are both smart and compounding. Try to resist the temptation to skip ahead without laying the right foundation. Utilize every tool and tax benefit that is available to you so you can maximize your cash flow and your ability to invest in your future and your children's future. Unfortunately, many people have no idea about the power of tax deferred savings plans and how much money they are leaving on the table by not taking advantage of them. Even more do not understand the difference between having a "rich" vs. a "wealthy" mindset. The wealthy continually invest their principal and live off the return, ensuring that they'll have resources to pass on. Meanwhile, the rich spend their principal and eventually go broke. Since there is no point in accumulating resources only to return to your former financial position as a result of poor spending habits, understanding the difference between a wealthy and a rich mindset is vitally important. Because African-Americans have such a small amount of intergeneration inheritance, there's a tremendous need to leave future generations with far more resources than previous generations inherited. But before you can do that you must understand that it is about more than how much you *make*, it's really about how much you *keep*. How much you make influences how much people *think* you have, how much you keep tells the truth about where you are financially. Knowing where you really are requires that you have a clear understanding of your current cash flow position, and the best way to do that is to create a fully burdened budget that lists all of your known *and* phantom expenses.

Focus on how to dramatically increase your current cash flow because, without positive cash flow, there can be no savings, no investment, no retirement, and certainly no foundation for wealth accumulation. *While most people focus on increasing income, reducing ex-penses has a far larger and more immediate impact on increasing cash flow.* But before any reductions are made you must understand the extent to which past experiences affect your current motives, values, and insecurities with respect to money and spending, and you should identify all negative multipliers. Be sure that you employ a mindset that always focuses on getting the highest value for the lowest price possible, wheth-er it's the cable bill, clothes, vacations, car purchases, or home purchases.

These efforts will dramatically increase your cash flow and position you to fund ownership and legacy. By using the debt waterfall method along with your in-cremental cash flow you can not only eliminate your debt in half the time, but you can also give yourself the equivalent of a 20% to 30% raise after your debt is eliminated. This in turn positions you to be able to save aggressively for retirement. It is a powerful con-tinuum and is what we mean by stewardship leads to ownership, which ultimately leads to legacy. Use your more in-depth understanding of credit, credit reports, and credit scores to reduce your cost of debt, which increases your cash flow and your ability to fund own-ership and legacy.

Understand that, at the end of the day, anything that continually reduces your ability to leave a legacy must be removed from your daily life and things that continually increase your ability to leave legacy are to be fostered, enhanced, and protected. You must always have a solid understanding of anything that affects legacy so you can be in the best position to augment or mitigate it.

Despite your focused and deliberate actions to leave a legacy for your children and their children, there have been, and there are still, significant headwinds faced by African-American families that continue to dramatically reduce our ability to leave a legacy. In my next book, *The Black Tax: The Cost of Being Black in America*, I quantify the economic cost of current and past discrimination against Black Americans; discuss how that cost continues to devastate our ability to leave a legacy, and lay out the steps you can take to help create the 6 million jobs and 1.4 million businesses that are missing in the Black community.

ABOUT THE AUTHOR

Shawn D. Rochester is an expert in identifying, optimizing, and allocating cash flow to help individuals, families, and organizations achieve their long-term financial goals. Shawn is a former corporate development and strategy executive who developed world-class cash flow management skills identifying and executing $500 million worth of transactions around the world and helping global business leaders generate over $10 billion of incremental revenue and cash flow.

Shawn spent the last 20 years developing what would become The Good Steward Financial Empowerment Series. Its powerful financial principles, based on stewardship, ownership, and legacy, have helped individuals and families dramatically increase their ability to maximize their cash flow, eliminate their debt and leave a legacy not only for their children, but also for their children's children. Shawn and his wife, Delores, founded Good Steward LLC (GSL) to provide financial education and advisory services based on the three core principles of stewardship, ownership, and legacy. Since founding GSL, Shawn has helped clients eliminate millions of dollars of debt, add tens of millions of assets to their retirement plans and position themselves to leave a greater legacy for their children's children than many clients thought possible.

Shawn holds a bachelor's degree in Chemical Engineering from The University of Rochester, and a master's degree in Business Administration from The University of Chicago Booth School of Business with a focus in Accounting, Finance, and Entrepreneurship. He lives in Southbury, Connecticut, with his wife and two children.

CPR For the SOuL is available on www.GoodStewardLiving.com

Visit www.GoodStewardLiving.com to order additional copies or for updates and events.

Or email the author at shawn.rochester@goodstewardllc.com

Connect with Shawn Rochester
Follow me on Facebook: GoodStewardLiving
Follow me on Twitter: rochester_shawn
Follow me Instagram: shawn.rochester
www.GoodStewardLiving.com

[i] http://www.demos.org/blog/11/5/13/racial-wealth-gap

[ii] "African Americans, Student Debt, and Financial Security," Demos, 2016, p. 2.

[iii] Low, David, "Quantifying Explanations for Black-White Wealth Inequality," March 2013, p. 8.

[iv] Proverbs 13:22, New International Version (NIV)

[v] Proverbs 16:16 NIV

[vi] Proverbs 4:7, King James Version (KJV)

[vii] Proverbs 24:7 NIV

[viii] Luke 16:10-12 NIV

[ix] Matthew 25:14-30 NIV

[x] One talent was equal to 6,000 denarii; 1 denarii is the wage for one day of work, 20.8 years to earn 6,000 denarii,

[xi] http://www.deptofnumbers.com/income/us/

[xii] https://www.google.com/amp/s/www.sbnation.com/platform/amp/nba/2016/7/2/12087368/nba-free-agency-2016-money-nfl-stars-explainer-andrew-luck-mike-conley

[xiii] https://www.si.com/vault/2009/03/23/105789480/how-and-why-athletes-go-broke

[ix] 30-year timeframe for goals = Short-term (first five years) + Mid-term (next 10 years) + Long-term (next 15 years)

[x] Five percent is an average annual return. It fluctuates from year to year. Some years it might be higher, some years lower but financial analysts generally expect a diversified portfolio of investments to generate about 5% per over the long-term

[xvi] $50,000 income minus the $5,000 invested in your company's 401k (or 403b plan for certain employees of public schools, employees of certain tax-exempt organizations, and certain ministers)

[xvii] $5,000 x 25%

[xviii] $5,000 + $2,000 +$1,250

[xix] National Center for Education Statistics – Degrees conferred by race and sex

[xx] Economic Policy Institute analysis of Federal Reserve survey data

[xxi] The crisis of economic insecurity for African-American and Latino Seniors

[xxii] Google Consumer Survey – December 2015

[xxiii] ROS = (Sales – Operating Expenses)/Sales

[xxiv] EBIT =Earnings Before Interest & Taxes

[xxv] Government Accountability Office – 2010 Large profitable companies paid an average effective tax rate of 16.9%

[xxvi] American Enterprise Institute – "The public thinks the average company makes 36% profit margin which is about 5x too high" April 2, 2015

[xxvii] American Economic Review 2015

[xxviii] http://taxfoundation.org/article/growing-class-americans-who-pay-no-federal-income-taxes

[xxix] http://floridarevenue.com/dor/property/brochures/pt110.pdf

[xxx] https://www.tax.ny.gov/pit/property/exemption/seniorexempt.htm

[xxxi]The credit is $3,000 for the care of one qualifying individual or $6,000 for two or more qualifying individuals. The amount of your credit is between 20 and 35 percent of your allowable expenses - IRS.Gov

[xxxii]Assumes full deduction of $2,550 at 25% tax rate

[xxxiii]USDA School Lunch and Breakfast Cost Study - II

[xxxiv]Economic Policy Institute

[xxxv]Brian Kluth - State of the Plate Research – Surveys from 4,413 tithers who tithe at least 10%

[xxxvi]NIV

[xxxvii]NIV Deuteronomy 28:12-13

[xxxviii]NIV Deuteronomy 28:43-44

[xxxix]NIV Proverbs 22:7

[xl]Average African-American pay 23% of income to debt. Assuming a 25% tax rate debt is actually consuming 30% of income on pretax basis

[xli]myFICO.com

[xlii]https://www.americanbanker.com/news/freddie-eyes-education-plan-as-study-finds-48-of-blacks-hampered-by
Researchers assigned a rating of "bad" to anyone who had two bills past due by more than 30 days in the past two years, a single bill past due by 90 days or more, a judgment against them, a lien against them or a bankruptcy

[xliii]An Overview and History of Credit Reporting 2002 - Mark Furletti

[xliv]http://www.myfico.com/CreditEducation/Questions/Credit_Problem_Comparison.aspx

[xlv]Experian data also show that consumers with the best credit scores utilize only 8% of their available credit – Nerdwallet.com

[xlvi]http://www.myfico.com/CreditEducation/Questions/Credit_Problem_Comparison.aspx

[xlvii]The Fair Credit Reporting Act (FCRA) requires each of the 3 Credit Bureaus (Equifax, Experian, and TransUnion) to provide you with a free copy of your credit report upon request annually.